Table of Contents

Table of Contents

Table of Contents

VEGGIE PIZZA

*M*ore exciting than routine vegetable sticks and dip, our Quick Vegetable Pizza is a cool treat for a friend. The munchable snack is easy to make — just bake purchased pizza dough, fill it with our tasty ranch-style spread, and top it with fresh veggies. Our recipe makes four pizzas, so there's plenty for you and several friends. Delivered in our clever "take-out" box, this gift is a vegetarian delight!

QUICK VEGETABLE PIZZAS

2 cans (10 ounces each) refrigerated pizza dough
1 cup sour cream
1 package (8 ounces) cream cheese, softened
1 package (0.4 ounces) ranch-style dressing mix
3 to 4 cups of any combination of the following raw vegetables shredded or cut into bite-size pieces: broccoli, squash, cherry tomatoes, carrots, green onions, sugar snap peas, radishes, mushrooms, red and green peppers, black olives, and cucumbers

Preheat oven to 350 degrees. Press dough into bottoms of four greased 9-inch round cake pans. Bake 15 to 20 minutes or until golden brown. Cool completely.

In a medium bowl, combine sour cream, cream cheese, and dressing mix. Spread sour cream mixture over pizza crusts. Place vegetables over sour cream mixture. Cover and store in refrigerator. Serve chilled.

Yield: four 9-inch pizzas

VEGGIE PIZZA BOX

For each box, you will need a 1³/₄" x 9¹/₄" x 9¹/₄" pizza take-out box, brown craft paper, 1³/₄"w craft ribbon, heavy white paper, red felt-tip pen with medium point, spray adhesive, and craft glue.

1. To cover top of box, use box lid as a pattern to cut a piece of craft paper; use spray adhesive to glue paper to lid.
2. (*Note:* Use craft glue for gluing in remaining steps.) Measure around sides of box; add ¹/₂". Cut a length of ribbon the determined measurement. Glue ribbon around sides of box.
3. Place pizza in box.
4. For banner, wrap ribbon diagonally around box with ends on bottom; glue ends to secure. Cut a 1¹/₄" x 9" strip of white paper. Use red pen to write "VEGGIE PIZZA" on paper. Glue paper to center of ribbon.

PEANUT BUTTER PIES

*H*ave *friends who
are nutty for peanuts? These
Crunchy Peanut Butter Pies
will be right up their alley!
Super-easy to make, the
no-bake treats have a fluffy
filling made with cream
cheese, peanut butter, and
non-dairy whipped topping.
Spoon the filling into little
graham cracker crusts for
neat individual portions,
garnish with peanuts, and
freeze until ready to present.
For delivery, decorate boxes
with wrapping paper, ribbon,
and artificial peanuts.*

CRUNCHY PEANUT BUTTER PIES

 1 package (8 ounces) cream cheese, softened
 2 cups sifted confectioners sugar
 3/4 cup crunchy peanut butter
 1 cup milk
 1 container (8 ounces) frozen non-dairy whipped topping, thawed
 18 tart-size or two 9-inch purchased graham cracker crusts
 1/2 cup chopped peanuts to garnish

In a large bowl, beat cream cheese until fluffy. Add confectioners sugar and peanut butter, beating until well blended. Gradually stir in milk. Fold whipped topping into cream cheese mixture; spoon into crusts. Garnish each pie with chopped peanuts. Freeze until firm. Store in an airtight container. Place in refrigerator about 30 minutes before serving.

Yield: 18 tart-size or two 9-inch pies

For each box, follow Gift Box instructions, page 122, to cover box with wrapping paper. We covered 8" pie boxes and decorated them with 2"w organdy ribbon, artificial peanuts, and greenery. For tag, use wrapping paper and follow Layered Tag instructions, page 122. Use black felt-tip pen with fine point to write "Crunchy Peanut Butter Pie" on tag.

8

LUSCIOUS FRUIT DRESSING

*T*his luscious Lemony *Fruit Salad Dressing is wonderful with apples, grapes, and other fresh fruits! It's super-easy to whip up with lemon yogurt and a few ingredients from your cupboard. For a presentation that will light up any fruit lover's eyes, place a jar of the creamy dressing in a basket lined with a cheerful cloth and tied with a citrus-trimmed bow. You'll want to add some fresh fruit too, so your friend can enjoy your gift right away.*

LEMONY FRUIT SALAD DRESSING

1 can (14 ounces) sweetened condensed milk
2 cups lemon-flavored yogurt
1/4 teaspoon salt
1/8 teaspoon ground white pepper

In a small bowl, combine all ingredients; stir until well blended. Store in an airtight container in refrigerator.

Yield: about 3 cups dressing

IN LOVE WITH CHOCOLATE

*M*ake your favorite chocoholic's dream come true with a gift of our easy-to-make Chocolate Lover's Snacks. Candy-coated chocolate pieces add a rainbow of color to bite-size cookies and chocolaty peanuts. For a sure way to brighten someone's day, present the concoction with a decorated cap!

CHOCOLATE LOVER'S SNACKS

- 1 package (10½ ounces) bite-size chocolate chip cookies
- 1 package (7½ ounces) bite-size chocolate sandwich cookies
- 1 package (6 ounces) candy-coated chocolate pieces
- 1 package (4½ ounces) chocolate-covered peanuts

In a large bowl, combine all ingredients. Store in an airtight container.

Yield: about 8 cups snacks

CHOCOLATE LOVER'S CAP

You will need a white fabric cap; white, red, and red print fabrics for hearts; 20" lengths of red and white ribbon and red metallic cord; red dimensional fabric paint in squeeze bottle; red glitter; brown permanent felt-tip pen with fine point; paper-backed fusible web; tracing paper; and safety pin.

1. For hearts, follow manufacturer's instructions to fuse web to wrong sides of fabrics. Trace heart patterns, page 119, onto tracing paper; cut out. Use patterns to cut 2 small hearts and 2 medium hearts from red print fabrics, 1 medium heart from white fabric, and 1 large heart from red fabric. Remove paper backing.
2. With white heart centered on large red heart, arrange hearts on bill of cap; fuse in place.
3. Use brown pen to write "I LOVE CHOCOLATE" on white heart.
4. Use red paint to paint around edge of large heart; before paint dries, sprinkle glitter over paint. Allow to dry; shake off excess glitter.
5. Tie ribbon and cord lengths together into a bow. Using safety pin on wrong side of cap, pin bow to top of cap.

10

AMARETTO ELEGANCE

*F*or a uniquely Italian treat, offer this delightful Amaretto Biscotti. These crunchy cookies, flavored with a subtle hint of amaretto and dipped in chocolate and nuts, make an elegant gift. And they're really easy to make with purchased zwieback toast! For delivery, pack the cookies in a decorative gift bag displaying Italy's national colors. Tie on a handwritten pennant for a completely irresistible package.

AMARETTO BISCOTTI

- 1 package (6 ounces) zwieback toast
- 4 tablespoons amaretto
- 6 ounces semisweet baking chocolate, chopped
- 1 tablespoon vegetable shortening
- 1 1/4 cups finely chopped pecans

Place pieces of toast on waxed paper. Spoon 1/2 teaspoon amaretto evenly over each piece of toast. Let stand 1 minute.

In a small saucepan, melt chocolate and shortening over low heat, stirring constantly. Remove from heat. Holding each piece of toast over saucepan, spoon chocolate over one-half of toast. Roll chocolate-covered end of toast in pecans. Return toast to waxed paper. Allow chocolate to harden. Store in an airtight container in a cool, dry place.

Yield: about 2 dozen cookies

For pennant, trace pennant and triangle patterns, page 118, onto tracing paper; cut out. Use pennant pattern to cut 1 pennant from red wrapping paper. Use triangle pattern to cut 1 triangle each from poster board and white paper. Matching points, use craft glue to glue poster board triangle to back of pennant. Trim 1/8" from edges of paper triangle. Center and glue paper triangle to front of pennant. Use a black felt-tip pen with fine point to write "amaretto biscotti" on pennant. Glue tab of pennant around 1 end of a wooden skewer. Use ribbon to tie pennant to bag.

*Y*ou can help your friends beat the heat this summer with a gift of our fabulous Peach Sours. A tangy blend of peach, orange, and lemon flavors, the fruity potion will be a hit at any gathering. For the perfect finishing touch, include a set of needlework coasters featuring an old-fashioned floral design.

PEACH SOURS

1 can (12 ounces) frozen lemonade concentrate, thawed
1 can (12 ounces) frozen orange-peach concentrate, thawed
1½ cups water
1½ cups peach brandy
Peach slices to garnish

Combine first 4 ingredients in a 2-quart container. Serve over ice; garnish with peach slices.

Yield: about eight 6-ounce servings

SUMMERTIME COASTERS

For each coaster, you will need a 3³/₈" square of 14 mesh plastic canvas, #20 tapestry needle, DMC embroidery floss (see color key), a 3" square of white felt, and craft glue.

1. Follow chart and use Tent Stitch, page 123, to work coaster. Complete background with white Tent Stitches. Use white Overcast Stitches, page 123, to work edges of coaster. Use 12 strands of floss for Tent Stitch and Overcast Stitch.
2. Glue felt square to back of coaster; allow to dry.

SUMMERTIME COASTER (47 x 47 threads)

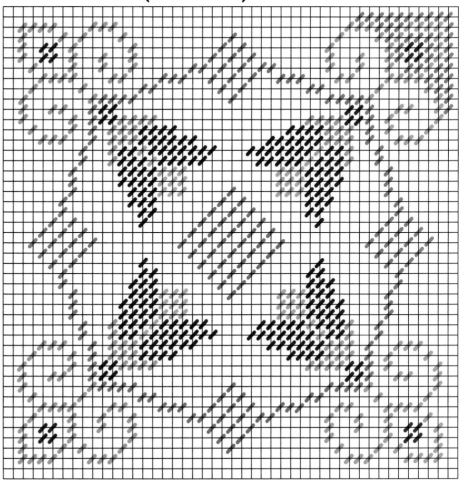

- ☑ white
- ☑ 562 green
- ☑ 727 yellow
- ☑ 3341 orange
- ☑ 3706 pink

*G*ive your new neighbors a warm welcome with our Potatoes au Gratin Casserole. Easy to prepare using a package of shredded potatoes, the cheesy dish will satisfy their hunger after a long day of unpacking. The "Welcome" spoon, with its cheery plaid house decoration and fabric tie, will remind them of your generosity long after you've become back-door buddies.

POTATOES AU GRATIN CASSEROLE

2 cups (8 ounces) shredded Cheddar cheese, divided
1 package (20 ounces) fresh shredded potatoes
1 cup sour cream
½ cup milk
1 jar (2 ounces) real bacon pieces
2 tablespoons butter or margarine, melted
1 teaspoon onion powder
½ teaspoon ground black pepper

In a 2-quart casserole, combine 1 cup cheese and remaining ingredients. Sprinkle remaining 1 cup cheese over top. Cover and store in refrigerator. Give with serving instructions.

Yield: about 8 servings

To serve: Bake uncovered in a preheated 350-degree oven about 45 minutes; cover and continue to bake 30 minutes or until heated through and cheese is bubbly.

"WELCOME" SPOON

You will need a wooden spoon, print fabric for house and tie, a 3" square of muslin for heart, a 4" square of poster board, black felt-tip pen with fine point, paper-backed fusible web, tracing paper, hot glue gun, and glue sticks.

1. For house, trace house and heart patterns onto tracing paper; cut out.
2. Cut a 4" square of print fabric. Follow manufacturer's instructions to fuse web to wrong sides of print fabric and muslin squares. Fuse print fabric square to poster board. Use patterns to cut house from fabric-covered poster board and heart from muslin. Fuse heart to center of house. Use pen to draw dashed lines around edge of heart to resemble stitches and to write "Welcome" on heart.
3. Hot glue house to spoon handle.
4. For tie, measure around casserole; add 14". Tear a 4"w strip of print fabric the determined measurement. Tie strip around casserole; tie ends of strip around spoon.

AN "AH SO" SWEET SAUCE

Confucius says: Good fortune awaits when you present a friend with our tangy Sweet and Sour Sauce! Easily prepared with a few purchased ingredients, it's delicious served warm or cold with Oriental food or hors d'oeuvres. Our recipe makes plenty, so you can share with several friends. For a delightful gift, pack a jar of the sauce in a take-out box covered with wrapping paper and add a sweet heart-shaped tag.

SWEET AND SOUR SAUCE

  1 jar (48 ounces) grape jelly
  3 bottles (12 ounces each) chili sauce
  1 jar (12 ounces) pineapple preserves
  ³/₄ cup firmly packed brown sugar
  6 tablespoons apple cider vinegar
  ³/₄ teaspoon ground ginger

In a large saucepan or Dutch oven, combine all ingredients over medium-high heat. Stirring frequently, cook until jelly melts and ingredients are well blended. Remove from heat. Store in an airtight container in refrigerator. Serve warm or cold with Oriental dishes, meats, or as a dipping sauce for hors d'oeuvres.

Yield: about 9 cups sauce

For covered box, follow Gift Box instructions, page 122. For tag, trace heart pattern, page 118, onto tracing paper; cut out. Use pattern to cut heart from pink paper. Use a purple calligraphy pen to write the following on tag: You "Ah So" Sweet.

Hot glue heart, silk flowers, and leaves to box. For jar lid, use flat part of jar lid as a pattern to cut a circle from pink paper. Use pen to write "Sweet and Sour Sauce" on circle. Place circle on jar lid; screw ring into place.

COOL MARGARITA PIE

Margarita fans will cheer for this unusual summertime dessert! Nestled in a pretzel crumb crust, the creamy filling for our Margarita Pies is prepared with tequila and purchased drink mixer. The recipe makes two tangy pies, so you can keep one for yourself, too! For a cool presentation, garnish the pie with lime slices and add a clever tag.

MARGARITA PIES

- 3 cups small pretzels, ground (about 1 1/2 cups crumbs)
- 2/3 cup butter or margarine, melted
- 1 envelope unflavored gelatin
- 1 cup liquid margarita mixer, divided
- 2 cans (14 ounces each) sweetened condensed milk
- 1/3 cup tequila
- 5 tablespoons orange-flavored liqueur
- 2 to 3 drops green food coloring
  Lime slices to garnish

For crusts, combine pretzel crumbs and butter in a small bowl. Press crumb mixture into bottom and up sides of two 8-inch pie pans. Place in refrigerator to chill.

In a microwave-safe measuring cup, sprinkle unflavored gelatin over 1/4 cup margarita mixer. Let mixture stand 2 minutes. Microwave on high power (100%) 40 seconds; stir thoroughly. Allow to stand 2 minutes or until gelatin is completely dissolved. In a large bowl, combine gelatin mixture, remaining 3/4 cup margarita mixer, condensed milk, tequila, liqueur, and food coloring until well blended and smooth. Divide filling equally between crusts; chill until firm. Garnish with lime slices. Cover and refrigerate.

Yield: two 8-inch pies

LUSCIOUS FRUIT HONEYS

FRUIT HONEYS

*T*opped with cute coordinating jar lids, our fruit-flavored honeys will make wonderful gifts for "beary" special friends. The condiments are simple to make by blending honey and cinnamon with strawberry preserves or blackberry jam, and they're great with homemade breads, biscuits, and more. Jars of the sweet treats are embellished with torn fabric bows and nestled in wooden berry crates.

STRAWBERRY HONEY
- ½ cup strawberry preserves
- 1 cup honey
- ⅛ teaspoon cinnamon

BLACKBERRY HONEY
- ½ cup seedless blackberry jam
- 1 cup honey
- ⅛ teaspoon cinnamon

For each fruit honey, microwave preserves or jam in a microwave-safe bowl on high power (100%) 1 minute or until melted. Stir honey and cinnamon into preserves until well blended. Store in an airtight container in refrigerator. Serve with breads, cereals, or baked fruits.

Yield: two fruit honeys about 1½ cups each

Note: If making "Beary" Jar Lids, store honeys in wide-mouth canning jars.

"BEARY" JAR LIDS

For each jar lid insert, you will need a 6½" square of ivory Aida (14 ct), embroidery floss (see color key), lightweight cardboard, polyester bonded batting, and craft glue.

1. Center and stitch desired design on Aida using 2 strands of floss for Cross Stitch, 2 for Backstitch lettering and DMC 676, and 1 for all other Backstitch.
2. To complete insert, follow Jar Lid Finishing, page 122.

X	DMC	¼X	B'ST	X	DMC	¼X	B'ST	X	DMC	¼X	B'ST
	ecru			✱	413				676		╱
	310	◢	╱	★	435	◢		✖	844		
	347	◢	╱	■	436	◢		♥	931	◢	
	367		╱	▲	437		□				
◆	368			★	646						

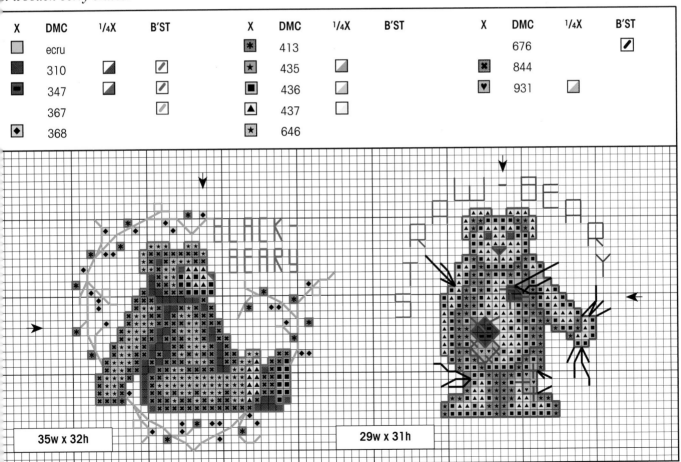

35w x 32h

29w x 31h

CAJUN POPCORN

*P*ut some spice into a friend's life with our Cajun Popcorn! To prepare it, simply toss plain popcorn with a buttery mixture of zesty seasonings and bake. In no time at all, you'll have a tangy snack that will give anyone's taste buds a workout! Yummy as a treat during the game or "just because," this Cajun concoction is sure to be a crowd-pleaser. A bandanna-lined basket trimmed with chili peppers makes an appropriate carrier for the spicy treat.

CAJUN POPCORN

- 1/2 cup butter or margarine, melted
- 2 teaspoons paprika
- 2 teaspoons lemon pepper
- 1 teaspoon salt
- 1 teaspoon garlic powder
- 1 teaspoon onion powder
- 1/4 teaspoon ground red pepper
- 20 cups popped popcorn

Preheat oven to 300 degrees. In a small bowl, combine butter, paprika, lemon pepper, salt, garlic powder, onion powder, and red pepper. Place popcorn in a large baking pan; pour butter mixture over popcorn and stir until well coated. Bake 15 minutes, stirring every 5 minutes. Remove from oven; cool completely. Store in an airtight container.

Yield: about 12 cups popcorn

BORDERS BOOKS - MUSIC - CAFE
1501 Fourth Ave. Seattle, WA 98101
(206) 622-4599
8343   0066/0003/03   000061   SALE
ITEM   TX RETAIL DISC SPEC   EXTND
QUICK GIFTS OF GOOD TASTE
1 IR 4796073 1   2.98   2.98
                 SUBTOTAL   2.98
    8.600%   TAX1   .26
1 Item   AMOUNT DUE   3.24
                ·CASH   3.24
                 CHANGE DUE   .00
        05/14/97   12:18 PM
Thank You For Shopping at Borders!
Opened CD, Tape, and Video product
is returnable ONLY if DEFECTIVE, and
for another copy of the same title.
            Thank you.

3 eggs, divided
1 package (18.25 ounces)
      chocolate butter cake mix
3/4 cup butter or margarine, softened
4 1/2 cups sifted confectioners sugar
1 package (8 ounces) cream cheese,
      softened
1 can (21 ounces) cherry pie filling

Preheat oven to 350 degrees. In a
large bowl, slightly beat one egg. Add
cake mix and butter; stir until well
blended. Press mixture into a greased
and floured 9 x 13-inch glass baking
dish. In a medium bowl, combine
confectioners sugar, cream cheese, and
remaining 2 eggs; pour over cake
mixture. Spread pie filling over cream
cheese mixture. Bake 30 to 40 minutes or
until outer edges are lightly browned
and center is almost set. Cool completely.
Cover and store in refrigerator. Serve at
room temperature.

Yield: about 24 servings

WELCOME BABY

*T*he birth of a baby is a
special time to celebrate.
During the first hectic days,
Mom will appreciate your
thoughtfulness in providing a
"welcome baby" dinner
featuring our creamy Poppy
Seed Chicken. And you won't
have to tell them how easy
it was to make the casserole
using deli chicken and
canned soup! Our generous
recipe makes two, so you
can keep one for yourself, too.
Nestled in our handy carrier,
made by stitching buttons to
the corners of a place mat,
the dish is perfect for
conveying your heartfelt
congratulations.

POPPY SEED CHICKEN

 1 package (12 ounces) spinach egg
   noodles
 2 tablespoons olive oil
 2 pounds thick-sliced delicatessen
   chicken breast, cut into bite-size
   pieces (about 6 cups)
 2 cans ($10^3/4$ ounces each) cream
   of chicken soup
$1^1/2$ cups sour cream
 1 can (8 ounces) sliced water
   chestnuts, drained
 $^1/2$ cup cooking sherry
 1 teaspoon dried tarragon leaves
 $^1/2$ teaspoon ground white pepper
 $^1/8$ teaspoon ground red pepper
 1 cup butter-flavored cracker crumbs
 2 teaspoons poppy seed
 6 tablespoons butter, melted

In a large saucepan, cook noodles
according to package directions. Drain
cooked noodles and toss with olive oil.
Place noodles in two 7 x 11-inch greased
glass baking dishes, spreading noodles up
sides of dishes. In a medium bowl, combine
chicken, soup, sour cream, water chestnuts,
sherry, tarragon, and peppers. Pour soup
mixture over noodles. Sprinkle cracker
crumbs and poppy seed over soup mixture.
Pour melted butter over crackers. Cover
and store in refrigerator. Give with serving
instructions.

Yield: 2 casseroles, about 6 servings each

To serve: Bake uncovered in a preheated
325-degree oven 55 to 60 minutes or until
heated through.

CASSEROLE CARRIER

*For a carrier to fit a 7" x 11" casserole
dish,* you will need a $12^1/2$" x $17^1/2$" place
mat (ours has angled corners), eight $^3/4$"
buttons, and thread to match place mat.

1. Position place mat wrong side up. Center
empty dish on place mat.
2. For each corner, fold edges of place mat
up and pin together at corner. Place 1
button on each side of corner close to dish.
Stitching through buttons and place mat,
sew buttons in place.

CUPCAKE CONES

These Ice-Cream Cone Cupcakes are as much fun to make as they are to eat! Simply fill ice-cream cones with chocolate cake batter (prepared from a mix), bake, and decorate with icing and candies. Perfectly sized for little hands, the festive treats are terrific for a child's birthday party or for classroom snacks. Delivered in cellophane-wrapped plastic cups, your creations will stay fresh until party time.

ICE-CREAM CONE CUPCAKES

CUPCAKES
- 1 package (18.25 ounces) chocolate cake mix
- 1¹/₄ cups water
- ¹/₂ cup vegetable oil
- 3 eggs
- 30 small flat-bottomed ice-cream cones

ICING
- 5 cups sifted confectioners sugar
- ³/₄ cup vegetable shortening
- ¹/₂ cup butter or margarine, softened
- 2¹/₂ tablespoons milk
- 1¹/₄ teaspoons almond extract

    Assorted purchased sprinkles and candies to decorate

For cupcakes, preheat oven to 350 degrees. In a large bowl, combine first 4 ingredients according to cake mix package directions. Fill each cone with about 2¹/₂ tablespoons of batter. Place cones about 3 inches apart on an ungreased baking sheet. Bake 25 to 30 minutes or until a toothpick inserted in center of cupcake comes out clean. Cool completely.

For icing, beat all ingredients together in a large bowl until smooth. Ice each cupcake with about 1 tablespoon icing. Before icing hardens, decorate with sprinkles and candies. Store in an airtight container.

Yield: 30 cupcakes

SNACK SACK

This Spicy Snack Mix, flavored with zesty taco seasoning, will add pizzazz to any couch potato's life! For a unique gift idea, package the mix in a burlap sack and tie it off with rope. A "Certified Couch Potato" pin adds just the right finishing touch to your presentation. This gift will be a hit any time of the year, and the recipe makes plenty for several gifts!

SPICY SNACK MIX

1/2 cup butter or margarine, melted
1 package (1.25 ounces) taco
   seasoning mix
4 cups cheese snack crackers
4 cups square corn cereal
2 1/2 cups (12 ounces) peanuts
2 cups small pretzels
2 cans (2.8 ounces each) french-
   fried onions

Preheat oven to 250 degrees. In a small bowl, blend butter and seasoning mix. In a large roasting pan, mix remaining ingredients. Pour butter mixture over snacks; stir until well coated. Bake 1 hour, stirring every 15 minutes. Cool completely. Store in an airtight container.

Yield: about 15 cups snack mix

COUCH POTATO SACK

You will need an 11" x 29" piece of burlap, 32" of 1/4" dia. rope, corrugated cardboard, cream-colored paper, tracing paper, graphite transfer paper, black felt-tip pen with medium point, brown colored pencil, pin back, drawing compass, and craft glue.

1. On 1 side of burlap, apply a line of glue close to each long edge. With glue sides together and matching short edges, fold burlap in half. Press glued edges together. Allow to dry.
2. Place a plastic bag of snack mix in bag.

3. Loosely tie rope around top of bag; knot rope ends.
4. For pin, cut a 4" dia. circle from cardboard and a 3 1/2" dia. circle from cream-colored paper. Trace potato pattern, page 118, onto tracing paper. Use transfer paper to transfer pattern to center of cream-colored paper. Use pen to draw over transferred lines and to color eyes and eyebrows. Use brown pencil to color potato. Glue paper to center of cardboard circle. Glue pin back to back of cardboard circle and allow to dry; pin to rope.

NUTTY ICE CREAM CRUMBLE

nutty
ice cream
crumble

*T*his Nutty Ice Cream Crumble topping transforms a plain dish of ice cream into a glorious dessert! The sweet, crunchy mixture of brown sugar, oats, and pecans is a delicious way to sprinkle some delight onto a favorite treat. For a tasty gift, package the topping in a homey fabric bag that's easy to make without sewing and include a jar of purchased ice cream sauce. A quilt block-inspired tag and a cozy fabric-lined basket make a charming presentation.

NUTTY ICE CREAM CRUMBLE

- 2 cups all-purpose flour
- 1 cup butter or margarine, softened
- 1 cup chopped pecans
- 1/2 cup firmly packed brown sugar
- 1/2 cup quick-cooking oats

Preheat oven to 400 degrees. In a medium bowl, combine all ingredients. Spread in an ungreased 10 x 15-inch jellyroll pan. Bake 15 minutes or until lightly browned, stirring once halfway through baking. Cool in pan. Store in an airtight container. Serve over ice cream topped with a purchased sauce.

Yield: about 5 cups topping

FABRIC BAG AND STAR TAG

For bag, you will need a 7" x 26" fabric piece, 1/2"w paper-backed fusible web tape, and 22" of 3/8"w satin ribbon.

For tag, you will need two 5" fabric squares, one 3" square of cream-colored paper, heavy paper, paper-backed fusible web, tracing paper, and a black felt-tip pen with fine point.

1. For bag, follow manufacturer's instructions to fuse a 13" length of web tape along 1/2 of each long edge on right side of fabric piece (Fig. 1). Remove paper backing.

Fig. 1

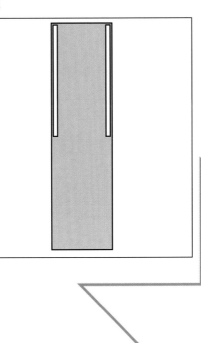

2. With right sides together and matching short edges, fold fabric in half; fuse side edges together.

3. Fuse a 7" length of web tape along top edge on each side of bag. Remove paper backing. Fold top edge of bag 3" to wrong side; fuse in place. Turn bag right side out.

4. Place a plastic bag of Nutty Ice Cream Crumble in fabric bag. Tie ribbon into a bow around top of bag.

5. For tag, fuse web to wrong sides of fabric squares and cream-colored paper. Remove paper backing. For star, fuse one 5" fabric square to heavy paper. Trace star pattern onto tracing paper; cut out. Use pattern to cut star from fabric-covered paper. For tag center, cut a 1 3/4" square from remaining 5" fabric square and fuse to center of fabric side of star. Cut a 1 3/8" square from cream-colored paper and fuse to center of fabric square. Use pen to write "nutty ice cream crumble" on tag.

COZY CASSEROLE

*C*ombining all the ingredients of the popular deli sandwich, our Hot Reuben Casserole is a hearty, satisfying dish that's perfect for greeting new neighbors. Tender corned beef, Thousand Island dressing, and Swiss cheese are layered on a bed of tangy sauerkraut and covered with crispy rye bread crumbs to make this filling entrée. Presented in our quick-and-easy casserole cozy, it's a delicious way to say, "Welcome, friends!"

HOT REUBEN CASSEROLE

- 2 cans (10 ounces each) chopped sauerkraut, drained
- 1 pound thinly sliced corned beef, coarsely chopped
- 3/4 cup Thousand Island dressing
- 8 ounces thinly sliced Swiss cheese
- 5 1/2 cups (about 8 ounces) coarsely crumbled rye bread
- 1/4 cup butter, melted

In a greased 8 x 11 1/2-inch baking dish, layer first 5 ingredients and drizzle with butter. Cover and store in refrigerator. Give with serving instructions.

Yield: about 6 to 8 servings

To serve: Bake uncovered in a preheated 375-degree oven 30 to 40 minutes or until casserole is heated through and bread crumbs are lightly browned.

CASSEROLE COZY

For cozy to hold an 8" x 11 1/2" dish, you will need two 13" x 17 1/4" quilted fabric place mats, thread to match place mats, three 7/8" dia. buttons, and three 3 1/2" lengths of 1/8"w elastic.

1. Position place mats wrong sides together. Leaving 1 short edge open, machine stitch place mats together along inner edge of binding.
2. For closure, evenly space buttons 1/2" from opening edge of top place mat; stitch in place. For each button loop, fold 1 length of elastic in half; sew ends of loop to inside edge of bottom place mat even with button (Fig. 1).

Fig. 1

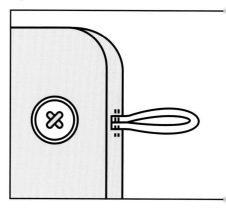

BITS OF SUNSHINE

*H*elp a friend look on the bright side with our sunny Lemon Bites. The tangy cookies are created with cake mix and coated with confectioners sugar. They're a sweet treat for a dreary day, especially when served with a cup of hot tea. Gift-wrapped in cellophane and tied with a bow, they'll bring a bit of sunshine to anyone's day.

LEMON BITES

    1   package (18.25 ounces)
            lemon-flavored cake mix
    1   egg
    1   container (4 ounces) frozen
            non-dairy whipped
            topping, thawed
   1/2 cup sifted confectioners sugar

Preheat oven to 350 degrees. In a large bowl, combine cake mix, egg, and topping (batter will be very stiff). Drop teaspoonfuls of dough into confectioners sugar. Roll into 1-inch balls, using sugar to keep dough from sticking to hands. Place balls of dough 2 inches apart on a greased baking sheet. Bake 10 to 12 minutes or until light brown on bottoms. Transfer to a wire rack to cool completely. Store in an airtight container.

Yield: about 6 dozen cookies

*P*ut a smile on your favorite youngster's face with a gift of bite-size Peanut Cream Sandwich Snacks. The chocolaty treats feature a fluffy filling of peanut butter, marshmallow creme, and a touch of honey sandwiched between bear-shaped graham snacks. For a "beary" special surprise, deliver a bag of the goodies with a cuddly bear pal sporting a colorful beanie and a bright bow tie.

PEANUT CREAM SANDWICH SNACKS

- 1/2 cup creamy peanut butter
- 1/4 cup marshmallow creme
- 1 tablespoon honey
- 1 package (10 ounces) chocolate bear-shaped graham snacks

In a small bowl, beat peanut butter, marshmallow creme, and honey with an electric mixer until well blended. Spoon mixture into a pastry bag fitted with a large round tip. Pipe about 1/4 teaspoon of peanut butter mixture onto 1 snack. Top with a matching bear shape. Repeat with remaining filling and snacks. Store in an airtight container.

Yield: about 100 snacks

PEANUT BUTTER BEAR

You will need a jointed teddy bear (ours is 11"h), a felt baseball cap to fit bear (available at craft stores), 2 colors of heavy paper for propellers on beanie, tracing paper, a 4mm bead, 8" of 7/8"w ribbon and 1" of 1/4"w ribbon for bow tie, thread to match ribbon, 1/8"w elastic, hot glue gun, and glue sticks.

1. For beanie, cut bill from cap; trim bottom edge of cap to fit bear's head.
2. Trace propeller pattern onto tracing paper; cut out. Use pattern to cut 1 propeller from each color of heavy paper.
3. Glue propellers to top of beanie; glue bead to center of propellers.
4. For bow tie, cut a 3 3/4" length of 7/8"w ribbon. Overlap ends 1/4" and tack together to form a loop. With overlap at center, flatten loop. Repeat with remaining 7/8"w ribbon. Matching centers, place small loop on large loop. Baste across center of loops. Pull basting thread, gathering loops at center; knot thread and trim ends. With ends at back, wrap 1/4"w ribbon around center of loops; tack in place.
5. Measure around bear's neck; cut a length of elastic the determined measurement. Thread elastic through back of bow. With bow at front, knot elastic around bear's neck; trim ends. Place beanie on bear's head.

QUICK QUESADILLAS CASSEROLE

*S*hare our Quesadillas Casserole, and share the spirit of a Mexican fiesta! Concealed beneath a bubbly topping of melted cheese, a well-seasoned bean mixture — easy to prepare with canned goods and spices — is nestled between flour tortillas and even more cheddar cheese! For a thoughtful gift idea, present the casserole and heating instructions to help out a friend who's having a busy day. A set of hand-stenciled recipe cards decorated with red peppers and a checkerboard border add a personal touch to your gift.

QUESADILLAS CASSEROLE

1 can (16 ounces) refried beans
1 can (8 ounces) tomato sauce
1 can (4 ounces) chopped green
   chilies
1 teaspoon ground cumin seed
1 teaspoon chili powder
1 teaspoon onion powder
1 teaspoon garlic powder
4 8-inch flour tortillas
   Vegetable cooking spray
2 cups (8 ounces) shredded
   Cheddar cheese, divided

In a small bowl, combine first 7 ingredients. Place 1 tortilla in an 8-inch round cake pan sprayed with vegetable cooking spray. Spread about 1/4 of bean mixture over tortilla. Repeat with second tortilla and bean mixture. Sprinkle 1 cup cheese over bean mixture. Repeat with remaining tortillas and bean mixture. Sprinkle remaining 1 cup cheese over top. Cover and refrigerate. Give with serving instructions.

Yield: about 8 servings

To serve: Bake uncovered in a preheated 350-degree oven 35 to 40 minutes or until heated through and cheese is bubbly.

STENCILED RECIPE CARDS

For each card, you will need 1 unlined 4" x 6" index card; acetate for stencils (available at craft or art supply stores); craft knife; cutting mat or thick layer of newspapers; removable tape (optional); red, green, and black acrylic paint; small stencil brushes; paper towels; and a black permanent felt-tip pen with fine point.

1. Referring to stencil cutting key and color key, follow Stenciling, page 122, to stencil design at top of index card.
2. Use pen to outline stems and chili peppers and to draw detail lines on chili peppers.
3. Use pen and a ruler to draw lines and dots on card 3/8" apart.

STENCIL CUTTING KEY
■ Stencil #1
▨ Stencil #2

COLOR KEY
Stencil #1 – red
Stencil #2 (stems) – green
Stencil #2 (checkerboard) – black

COCK-A-DOODLE CRUNCH

*D*on't be too chicken to share this crunchy corn snack with your plucky friends. Coated with a spicy seasoning, our Chicken Feed is especially easy to make, and it'll give your friends something to crow about at your next casual or country-theme party! For a cleverly "corny" conversation piece, fill a newly purchased chicken feeder with the mix and watch the fun begin.

CHICKEN FEED

2 packages (5.6 ounces each)
    crunchy toasted corn
2 tablespoons extra spicy salt-free
    seasoning
1 tablespoon vegetable oil

In a medium bowl, combine all ingredients; stir until corn is well coated. Store in an airtight container.

Yield: about 4 cups snacks

TEMPTING ALMOND BUTTER

*T*ry a new twist on peanut butter with our yummy Toasted Almond Butter! This creamy spread is so easy you'll have plenty of time to whip up some for a friend — and yourself, too! Simply blend toasted almonds and salt in a food processor, and in no time you'll have a delightful snack! Top a jar of the spread with a fabric-covered lid and deliver your present in a basket decorated with a coordinating bow, moss, and almonds.

TOASTED ALMOND BUTTER

   3 cups slivered almonds, toasted
   1 teaspoon salt

In a food processor, process almonds and salt until mixture has a buttery consistency. Store in an airtight container in refrigerator. Serve with crackers.

Yield: about 1 cup almond butter

For basket, hot glue Spanish moss, then almonds, to rim of basket. Tear a strip from fabric; tie strip into a bow. Hot glue bow to rim of basket. For jar lid, spray paint screw ring if desired; allow to dry. For insert, follow Jar Lid Finishing, page 122.

*M*oist and delicious, these Cinnamon-Apple Coffee Cakes will spice up break time! The old-fashioned treats taste like you baked all day, but they're really easy to make with purchased cake mix and apple pie filling. The recipe makes a dozen little cakes, so you can share them with your sewing group or friends at work. Perfect for carrying the cakes, our homey padded basket is simple to create without sewing — the fabric is secured with a rubber band!

CINNAMON-APPLE COFFEE CAKES

- 3/4 cup crushed cinnamon graham crackers (about five 2 1/2 x 5-inch crackers)
- 3/4 cup chopped walnuts
- 2 teaspoons ground cinnamon
- 1 package (16 ounces) pound cake mix
- 1 can (21 ounces) apple pie filling
- 2 eggs, beaten
- 2 tablespoons sour cream

Preheat oven to 325 degrees. In a small bowl, mix crushed crackers, walnuts, and cinnamon. In a large bowl, combine cake mix, pie filling, eggs, and sour cream; beat with an electric mixer until well blended. Spoon 1 tablespoon graham cracker mixture into bottom of each greased and floured tin of a 6-mold fluted tube pan. Spoon 2 rounded tablespoons batter over cracker mixture. Spoon 1 tablespoon cracker mixture over batter. Top with 2 tablespoons batter. Bake 45 to 50 minutes or until toothpick inserted into center of cake comes out clean. Cool in pan 5 minutes; invert cakes onto a wire rack and cool completely. Store in an airtight container.

Yield: twelve 4-inch coffee cakes

EASY COVERED BASKET

You will need a round basket; fabric to cover basket; polyester bonded batting; rubber band to fit around basket; preserved cedar; artificial fruit, nuts, and greenery; cinnamon sticks; florist wire; masking tape; hot glue gun; and glue sticks.

1. Referring to Fig. 1, measure basket from rim to rim; add 7". Cut a circle of fabric the determined measurement.

Fig. 1

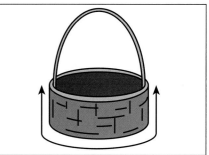

2. For padding, measure height of basket and subtract 1"; measure around outside of basket. Cut a strip of batting the determined measurements. With 1 long edge of batting along bottom edge of basket, wrap batting around outside of basket; glue to secure.
3. Center basket on wrong side of fabric circle. Bring edge of fabric to inside of basket and secure with tape. Place rubber band around basket 1" from rim. Remove tape and roll edge of fabric to wrong side, tucking edge of fabric under rubber band.
4. Cross cinnamon sticks and wire together; glue preserved cedar, greenery, fruit, and nuts to cinnamon sticks. Wire arrangement to basket handle.

KID-PLEASING POPCORN CAKE

*S*ay "Happy Birthday" to a favorite youngster with a colorful Popcorn Cake. A kid-pleasing mixture of popcorn, peanuts, candy-coated chocolate chips, and marshmallows, the "cake" is shaped in a tube pan and decorated with gum ball "balloons" with icing strings. More gum balls are poured in the center hole of the cake to hold an arrangement of real balloons tied to drinking straws. What a fun addition to a party!

POPCORN CAKE

 1 package (16 ounces) regular marshmallows
 ½ cup butter or margarine
 ¼ cup vegetable oil
 16 cups popped popcorn
 1 can (12 ounces) salted peanuts
 ½ cup candy-coated mini chocolate chips

Small balloons, plastic drinking straws, gum balls, and purchased decorating icing to decorate

In a large saucepan over medium heat, combine marshmallows, butter, and oil; stir constantly until marshmallows are melted. Place popcorn and peanuts in a very large bowl; stir in marshmallow mixture. Add chocolate chips; lightly stir into popcorn mixture. Press popcorn mixture into a greased 10-inch tube pan; pack firmly. Place in refrigerator 30 minutes or until set. Unmold onto a serving plate.

To decorate cake, pipe decorating icing onto cake for balloons strings; place a gum ball at one end of each string. Blow up balloons and tie onto end of straws; place in opening of cake. Fill opening with gum balls.

Yield: about 12 servings

Fast Fiesta Fare

*F*or a spicy surprise, present all the fixin's for a bowl of fresh, chunky salsa. Our flavorful Salsa Mix — a combination of cilantro, garlic, onion, and sweet pepper flakes — is ready to add to a can of stewed tomatoes for a mild snack. Blended with diced tomatoes and green chilies, it makes a sassier sauce. To add to the fun, include crispy chips and a painted dish — it's easy to make with a clay flowerpot saucer!

SALSA MIX

1 1/2 cups dried cilantro
  1/4 to 1/2 cup garlic powder
  1/2 cup dried chopped onion
  1/2 cup dried sweet pepper flakes
    2 tablespoons salt
    2 tablespoons ground black pepper

In a small bowl, combine all ingredients until well blended. Store in an airtight container. Give with serving instructions.

Yield: about 2 3/4 cups mix

To serve: For a spicy salsa, blend 2 tablespoons salsa mix with one 10-ounce can diced tomatoes and green chilies. For a mild salsa, blend 2 tablespoons salsa mix with one 14 1/2-ounce can stewed tomatoes that have been finely chopped. Serve salsa with chips. For a spread, blend 2 tablespoons salsa mix with 1 cup softened cream cheese and serve with crackers. Refrigerate all prepared mixtures overnight to allow flavors to blend.

For salsa dish, use a pencil to lightly draw letters and designs on rim of a terra-cotta flowerpot saucer. Use a black permanent felt-tip pen with medium point and yellow, red, and turquoise dimensional paint pens to go over letters and designs; allow paint to dry. (*Note:* Use for dry foods only. Wipe clean with a damp cloth.)

CRUNCHY CHOCOLATE CANDIES

*O*nly *have a few
minutes? Great! Because
that's all you'll need to stir
up a batch of Crunchy
Chocolate Candies. This
extra-easy two-ingredient
confection is made with
crispy rice cereal and
chocolate-flavored candy
coating. Placed in tiny foil
cups, the candies make
tasteful last-minute gifts
for any occasion! To make
your offering more special,
package the sweets in
purchased candy boxes tied
with coordinating ribbons.*

CRUNCHY CHOCOLATE
CANDIES

14 ounces chocolate-flavored candy
      coating
2¹/₂ cups crispy rice cereal

In a heavy medium saucepan, melt candy
coating over low heat. Stir in cereal. Drop
by tablespoonfuls into foil candy cups. Place
candies in refrigerator to harden. Store in
an airtight container in refrigerator.

Yield: about 3¹/₂ dozen candies

A Taste Of The Orient

*I*f you believe that variety is the spice of life, then you'll love sharing our unusual Oriental Salad Dressing with like-minded friends. Simply combine rice vinegar, sesame oil, and Chinese five spice powder with a few pantry staples and, in minutes, you've got it made. Perfect for spicing up a plain salad, the dressing will add Oriental style to any meal. Along with the jar of dressing, include a set of Chinese bowls and some chopsticks for an especially nice gift.

ORIENTAL SALAD DRESSING

- 1 cup vegetable oil
- 3/4 cup rice vinegar
- 1/4 cup plus 2 tablespoons sugar
- 1/4 cup dark sesame oil
- 2 tablespoons dry mustard
- 2 teaspoons salt
- 1 teaspoon Chinese five spice powder

Combine all ingredients in a 1-quart jar with a tight-fitting lid. Shake until well blended. Store in refrigerator. Serve with salad or stir-fried vegetables.

Yield: about 2 1/4 cups dressing

Warm up a cold winter's day with a rich, steaming bowl of Cheesy Corn Chowder. A hearty blend of canned potato and Cheddar cheese soups with cream-style corn, it's super-easy to stir together! For a delicious gift that's sure to put stars in a friend's eyes, present the powder in a fabric-topped jar. A star-studded place mat and coordinating tag are thoughtful additions to your presentation. They're easy to paint with foam stamps, and the "stitching" is done with a felt-tip pen!

CHEESY CORN CHOWDER

- 2 cans (17 ounces each) yellow cream-style corn
- 1 can (10³/₄ ounces) cream of potato soup, undiluted
- 1 can (10³/₄ ounces) Cheddar cheese soup, undiluted
- ½ cup real bacon pieces (½ of a 2-ounce jar)
- 2 cups milk
- 2 teaspoons dried chopped onion
- 1 teaspoon dried parsley flakes
- ¼ teaspoon ground red pepper

In a large saucepan, combine all ingredients. Stirring occasionally, cook soup on medium-high heat until heated through. Store in an airtight container in refrigerator.

Yield: about 8 cups soup

PLACE MAT AND JAR TOPPER

For each place mat, you will need a fabric place mat, ¹/₁₆" thick crafting foam, two 2" square wood pieces cut from a 2 x 4, brown permanent felt-tip pen with fine point, blue and yellow acrylic paint, paintbrush, tracing paper, hot glue gun, and glue sticks.

For jar topper and tag, you will *also* need a 2¹/₄" x 4¹/₂" piece of cream-colored paper, fabric to cover jar lid, raffia, pinking shears, a rubber band, and a hole punch.

1. For stamps, trace patterns onto tracing paper; cut out. Use patterns to cut shapes from crafting foam. Glue 1 shape to each wood piece.

2. To paint place mat, use paintbrush to apply blue paint to square stamp and yellow paint to star stamp. Alternating stamps and reapplying paint as necessary, use stamps to stamp squares and stars along each short edge of place mat. Allow to dry.

3. Use pen to draw dashed lines on each square and around each star to resemble stitching.

4. For jar topper, use pinking shears to cut a circle of fabric 2" larger all around than jar lid. Center fabric circle right side up on jar lid. Wrap rubber band around fabric circle to secure circle to jar. Tie raffia into a bow around fabric circle, covering rubber band.

5. For tag, fold paper in half, matching short edges. Use paintbrush to apply yellow paint to star stamp. Use stamp to stamp star on front of tag; allow to dry. Use pen to draw dashed lines around star to resemble stitching. Punch a hole in tag. Thread tag onto raffia.

ROCKY ROAD CLASSIC

*T*he man in your life will be thrilled with a gift of Microwave Rocky Road Fudge! This classic confection requires only a handful of ingredients and whips up fast in the microwave. In no time, you'll have a chocolaty, marshmallowy delight that's too good to keep to yourself! Our handsome tin, dressed in a rich paisley print, is just right for delivering your sweet chocolate surprise.

MICROWAVE ROCKY ROAD FUDGE

4$^{1}/_{2}$	cups sifted confectioners sugar
$^{1}/_{2}$	cup butter or margarine
$^{1}/_{3}$	cup cocoa
$^{1}/_{4}$	cup milk
$^{1}/_{4}$	teaspoon salt
$^{1}/_{2}$	cup chopped pecans
$^{1}/_{2}$	cup miniature marshmallows
1	teaspoon vanilla extract

In a large microwave-safe bowl, combine confectioners sugar, butter, cocoa, milk, and salt. Microwave on high power (100%) 2 to 2$^{1}/_{2}$ minutes or until butter is melted. Add pecans, marshmallows, and vanilla; stir until well blended. Pour into an 8-inch square pan lined with greased aluminum foil. Refrigerate about 1 hour or until firm. Cut into 1-inch squares and store in an airtight container.

Yield: about 1$^{1}/_{2}$ pounds fudge

FABRIC-COVERED TIN

You will need a round tin canister with lid (we used a 4" dia. x 5$^{1}/_{2}$"h canister), fabric to cover canister and lid, fabric with motif for appliqué, satin ribbon same width as side of lid, $^{1}/_{4}$"w grosgrain ribbon, $^{1}/_{16}$" dia. twisted gold cord, polyester bonded batting, fabric marking pencil, spray adhesive, craft glue, and spring-type clothespins.

1. To cover canister, leave lid on canister and measure from bottom edge of lid to bottom edge of canister; add 1". Measure around side of canister; add 1". Cut a piece of fabric the determined measurements. Remove lid from canister.

2. (*Note:* Use craft glue for all gluing unless otherwise indicated.) Press each long edge and 1 short edge of fabric piece $^{1}/_{2}$" to wrong side. Apply spray adhesive to wrong side of fabric. Beginning with unpressed short edge and with 1 long edge of fabric along bottom edge of canister, smooth fabric onto canister. Glue pressed edge at overlap to secure.

3. (*Note:* To prevent ends of cord from fraying after cutting, apply glue to $^{1}/_{2}$" of cord around area to be cut, allow to dry, and then cut.) For appliqué, cut a circle from fabric with desired motif at center. Use spray adhesive to glue appliqué to front of canister. Beginning at bottom, glue cord along edge of appliqué, trimming to fit exactly.

4. Leaving ends unglued, cut a 5" length of cord. Tie a loose double knot at center of cord; knot each end $^{3}/_{4}$" from ends and fray ends. Glue double knot at bottom of appliqué.

5. To cover lid, use fabric marking pencil to draw around lid on wrong side of fabric. Cut out fabric $^{1}/_{2}$" outside pencil line. Clip edge of fabric at $^{1}/_{2}$" intervals to within $^{1}/_{8}$" of line. Use top of lid as a pattern and cut a circle from batting. Glue batting to lid. Center fabric circle right side up on lid. Alternating sides and pulling fabric taut, glue clipped edges of fabric to side of lid; secure with clothespins until glue is dry. If necessary, trim edges of fabric just above bottom of lid.

6. Measure around side of lid; add $^{1}/_{2}$". Cut a length from each ribbon the determined measurement. Glue satin ribbon to side of lid; center and glue grosgrain ribbon over satin ribbon.

HERBED BUTTERS

*B*utter up your
favorite cook with one of
these sensational seasoned
spreads. One pat of Garlic-
Pepper Butter makes a good
steak simply superb, and
the Lemon-Dill Butter
(shown) adds a refreshingly
delightful flavor to fish.
You can whip up the tasty
condiments in minutes
and present them attractively
attired in fabric wraps tied
with jute bows.

SEASONED ROLLED BUTTERS

GARLIC-PEPPER BUTTER

- 1 cup butter, softened
- 5 to 6 cloves minced garlic *or*
  - ³/4 teaspoon garlic powder
- 1 tablespoon finely chopped fresh parsley *or* 1 teaspoon dried parsley flakes
- 1 tablespoon lemon juice
- ¹/2 teaspoon salt
- ¹/2 teaspoon ground white pepper

LEMON-DILL BUTTER

- 1 cup butter, softened
- 2 tablespoons lemon juice
- 1 tablespoon grated lemon zest
- 1 teaspoon dried dill weed

For each seasoned butter, whip butter with an electric mixer in a small bowl until smooth and fluffy. Continue to beat, gradually adding remaining ingredients. Using waxed paper, shape butter mixture into a 6-inch-long log. Store in refrigerator. Serve garlic-pepper butter on steaks, fish, vegetables, and pastas. Serve lemon-dill butter on fish, vegetables, and pastas.

Yield: two 1-cup butter rolls

FABRIC BUTTER WRAPS

For each wrap, you will need a 7" x 12" torn fabric piece, a 6" square of lightweight cardboard, two 14" lengths of 3-ply jute, ⁵/8"w paper-backed fusible web tape, and transparent tape.

For optional stenciling, you will *also* need a 1"h lettering stencil, fabric paint, stencil brush, paper towels, removable tape, and a black permanent felt-tip pen with fine point.

1. (*Note:* If desired, follow Step 1 to stencil "butter" lengthwise at center on right side of fabric piece.) Use tape to mask any cutout areas on stencil next to area being painted. Hold or tape stencil in place. Use a clean, dry stencil brush. Dip brush in paint and remove excess on a paper towel. Brush should be almost dry to produce good results. Beginning at edge of cutout area, apply paint in a stamping motion. Carefully remove stencil and allow paint to dry. Use pen to outline letters.
2. Follow manufacturer's instructions to fuse web tape along 1 long edge on wrong side of fabric piece. Overlap webbed edge ⁵/8" over remaining long edge to form a tube; fuse edges together.
3. Roll cardboard into a tube, overlapping edges ¹/2"; tape overlapped edges together.
4. Insert cardboard tube into fabric tube. Gather fabric at one end of tube; tie 1 length of jute into a bow around fabric to secure. Place wrapped butter roll inside tube. Gather fabric at remaining end of tube and tie with remaining jute.

CUP OF CHEER

*O*ur Hot Buttered *Drink Mix makes it easy to "sip" into the holiday spirit with a warm cup of cheer. This flavorful concoction of butter, brown sugar, and spices is stirred into apple cider to create a wonderful treat for the holiday season. A shot of rum can be added to the spicy drink for extra flavor. To surprise a friend, deliver a ribbon-tied bag of the mix in a decorative mug.*

HOT BUTTERED DRINK MIX

2³/₄   cups firmly packed brown
        sugar
   1   cup unsalted butter, softened
   3   tablespoons maple syrup
   6   teaspoons ground cinnamon
2¹/₂   teaspoons ground cloves
 ³/₄   teaspoon ground nutmeg

In a medium bowl, combine all ingredients with an electric mixer until well blended. Store in an airtight container in refrigerator. Give with serving instructions.

Yield: about 3 cups mix

To serve: Stir 1¹/₂ teaspoons drink mix into 6 ounces of hot apple cider or other juices. For hot buttered rum, add 1 ounce rum to cider mixture.

GARDEN CHILI

*A*dd a bit of zing to a neighbor's lunch with our hearty Vegetarian Chili. Loaded with scrumptious garden favorites, it's really quite easy to make using frozen and canned vegetables. Our simple hand-painted bowls and a jar of the spicy mixture make a great gift for someone who just wants to "Veg Out!"

VEGETARIAN CHILI

- 1 package (16 ounces) frozen vegetable gumbo mix (okra, corn, celery, onion, and sweet red pepper)
- 2 cans (16 ounces each) pinto beans, undrained
- 2 cans (15 ounces each) black beans, undrained
- 2 cans (14½ ounces each) stewed tomatoes
- 1 can (4 ounces) chopped green chilies, undrained
- 2 tablespoons chili powder
- 1 tablespoon sugar
- ¾ teaspoon salt
- ¼ teaspoon ground red pepper

In a Dutch oven over medium-high heat, combine all ingredients. Stirring occasionally, bring to a boil. Reduce heat to medium-low; simmer 20 to 30 minutes.

Yield: about 12 cups chili

"VEG OUT!" CHILI BOWLS

For each bowl, you will need a ceramic bowl; orange, Christmas red, and Christmas green DecoArt™ Ultra Gloss™ Acrylic Enamel paint; a liner brush; and small round paintbrushes.

1. Wash and dry bowl.
2. Use a pencil to lightly write "VEG OUT!" on bowl.

3. (*Note:* Allow to dry after each paint color.) Use liner brush to paint letters red. Use small round paintbrush to paint orange carrots and green carrot tops on bowl.
4. Follow paint manufacturer's instructions to cure paint and to wash finished bowl.

*S*teeped in a savory sauce of vinegar, oil, herbs, and spices, colorful green and ripe olives are perfect pick-me-ups for a party relish tray. For a distinctly Greek flavor, the zesty Marinated Spiced Olives are great sprinkled over a tossed salad, too! Add an easy-to-make "tuxedo" label and a cute message to the jar, and you'll have a wonderful gift for your dinner hostess.

MARINATED SPICED OLIVES

1 can (7¼ ounces) large whole unpitted ripe olives, drained
1 jar (5 ounces) whole unpitted green olives, drained
¾ cup olive oil
5 cloves garlic, halved
¼ small onion, thinly sliced
3 tablespoons tarragon vinegar
1 teaspoon cumin seed
1 teaspoon coriander seed

In a small bowl, combine all ingredients; stir until olives are well coated. Store in an airtight container in refrigerator. Allow flavors to blend 3 days, stirring each day. Bring to room temperature to serve.

Yield: about 3 cups olives

"OLIVE" YOUR STYLE JAR

You will need a jar at least 6"h, white paper, black felt-tip pen with fine point, three ¼" dia. black buttons, 9" of 2"w wired ribbon, 2½" of 1½"w plaid ribbon, satin ribbon same width as neck of jar, hot glue gun, and glue sticks.

1. Use black pen to trace shirt pattern onto paper; cut out.
2. Glue shirt to jar. Glue buttons to shirt.
3. For tie, begin at center front and glue satin ribbon around neck of jar, trimming to fit. Overlap ends of 2"w ribbon 1" to form a loop; glue ends together. With overlap at back, flatten loop. Press long edges of 1½"w ribbon ¼" to wrong side. With wrong side of ribbon facing loop, wrap pressed ribbon around center of loop, overlapping ends at back; glue to secure. Glue bow to satin ribbon on jar.

A GARDEN-FRESH GIFT

*T*his garden-fresh gift will delight anyone who loves the goodness of summer vegetables. You can include veggies from your garden or the farmers' market, along with a jar of cool Cucumber-Garlic Dip for healthy munching. The extra-easy dip starts with cheeses and salad dressing mix. Colorful seed packets (saved from previous plantings) are a fun, inexpensive way to trim your basket. To inspire your friend's green thumb, include a pair of gardening gloves — you can even turn one into a "bow" using our easy technique.

CUCUMBER-GARLIC DIP

 1 large cucumber, peeled and
    quartered
 1 container (8 ounces) cottage
    cheese
 1 package (8 ounces) cream cheese,
    softened
 1 cup chopped pecans
 1 package (0.4 ounces) ranch-style
    salad dressing mix
 2 teaspoons garlic powder
 2 teaspoons onion powder
    Fresh vegetables to serve

In a blender or food processor, combine all ingredients; process until cucumber and pecans are puréed. Cover and refrigerate until well chilled. Serve with fresh vegetables.

Yield: about 3¹/₂ cups dip

For basket, hot glue 1"w craft ribbon around basket. Hot glue empty seed packets to basket over ribbon. For glove bow, fanfold 1 garden glove lengthwise, leaving thumb free; knot an 18" length of jute around center of glove. Wrap thumb around center of glove, covering jute; tack in place. Use ends of jute to tie glove bow to basket handle. Place remaining glove in basket.

FIERY HOT DOG RELISH!

*W*e awarded four stars to our three-alarm Fiery Mustard Relish, a sizzling combination of jalapeño mustard, dill pickles, and spices. This crunchy condiment is perfect for folks who like their dogs hot! A "flaming" paper sleeve transforms an ordinary jar into a novel presentation for someone who's "hot stuff"!

FIERY MUSTARD RELISH

  1 jar (32 ounces) dill pickle slices, drained
  1/2 cup prepared jalapeño mustard
  1 teaspoon minced dried onion
  1/2 teaspoon garlic powder

Combine all ingredients in a food processor; pulse process 4 or 5 times or until mixture is coarsely chopped. Store in an airtight container in refrigerator.

Yield: about 2 1/2 cups relish

"HOT STUFF" JAR

You will need a jar (our jar measures 4 1/4"h x 4" dia.); yellow, orange, red, and black paper; black felt-tip pen with medium point; craft glue; and a drawing compass.

1. Measure height of jar. Measure around jar; add 1/2". Cut a strip of black paper the determined measurements.

2. For flames, cut 1 strip each of yellow, orange, and red paper the same length and 3/4 the width of the black strip. Use a pencil to draw flames along 1 long edge on wrong side of red strip; cut out. Matching straight long edge (bottom) of red strip to 1 long edge of orange strip, place red strip on orange strip; cut orange strip approx. 1/8" larger than red strip. Using orange strip as a pattern, repeat to cut flames from yellow

strip. Matching bottom edges, glue strips together.

3. Matching bottom edge of flames to 1 long edge of black strip, glue flames to black strip. Overlapping short edges, wrap black strip around jar and glue in place.

4. For top of jar, cut a circle from yellow paper to fit center of lid. Use pen to write "HOT STUFF" on circle. Glue circle to lid.

Amaretto-Nut Cherry Sauce

Your friends will cheer for this Amaretto-Nut Cherry Sauce! The quick-and-easy concoction is made with cherry preserves, slivered almonds, and just a hint of almond liqueur. The sweet, fruity topping is also great over pudding or cake. Delivered in our appliquéd bag, this divine dessert addition is just the right gift for satisfying a sweet tooth.

AMARETTO-NUT CHERRY SAUCE

 2 jars (18 ounces each) cherry preserves
 2 tablespoons firmly packed brown sugar
 1 cup slivered almonds, toasted
 1/4 cup amaretto

In a medium saucepan, combine preserves and brown sugar over medium heat. Stirring occasionally, cook until sugar dissolves. Remove from heat; stir in almonds and amaretto. Store in an airtight container in refrigerator. Serve warm or cold with ice cream, pudding, or cake.

Yield: about 4 cups sauce

CHERRY BAG

You will need a 7" x 21" fabric piece for bag, thread to match fabric, red fabric for cherries, brown fabric for stems, green fabric for leaves, a 1" x 25" torn fabric strip for tie, paper-backed fusible web, and tracing paper.
For tag, you will *also* need fabric, white paper, heavy paper, embroidery floss, black felt-tip pen with fine point, craft glue, and a 1/8" hole punch.

1. For bag, follow Steps 2 and 4 of Fabric Bag instructions, page 122. Fringe top of bag 1/4".

2. For appliqué, follow manufacturer's instructions to fuse web to wrong sides of fabric pieces for cherries, stems, and leaves. Trace cherry, stem, and leaf patterns onto tracing paper; cut out. Use patterns to cut 2 cherries, 2 stems, and 1 of each leaf from fabric pieces. Remove paper backing.
3. Arrange stems, cherries, and leaves on front of bag; fuse in place.
4. Place jar of sauce in bag. Tie torn fabric strip into a bow around top of bag.
5. For tag, follow Layered Tag instructions, page 122. Use pen to write "Amaretto-Nut Cherry Sauce" on tag. Punch hole in tag. Use floss to tie tag to bag.

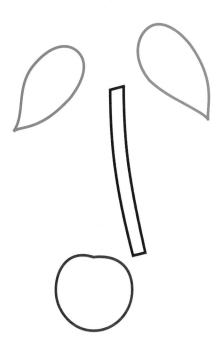

EASY PEACH FREEZER JAM

*S*hare the summery goodness of peaches any time of the year with luscious Peach Freezer Jam. So much easier to make than traditional jams, this sweet condiment is made with frozen sliced peaches and prepared with the help of a microwave! It keeps for up to a year in the freezer, so you can have it on hand when you need a quick treat. To deliver your surprise, pack the jam in jars dressed up with peach-stenciled lids and homespun fabric bows. The lucky recipient of this gourmet gift will think you're a real peach.

PEACH FREEZER JAM

- 1 package (16 ounces) frozen peach slices, thawed
- 1 package (3 ounces) peach-flavored gelatin
- 2 tablespoons lemon juice
- 1/2 teaspoon ascorbic powder (used to preserve fruit color)
- 4 1/2 cups sugar
- 3/4 cup water
- 1 package (1 3/4 ounces) pectin powder

In a food processor, combine peach slices, gelatin, lemon juice, and ascorbic powder; pulse process until peaches are finely chopped. In a large bowl, combine sugar and fruit mixture; let stand 10 minutes. In a 1-quart microwave-safe bowl or measuring cup, combine water and pectin; microwave on high power (100%) 2 to 2 1/2 minutes or until mixture boils. Microwave another 45 seconds; stir. Microwave 15 seconds longer; stir. Pour hot pectin mixture into fruit mixture; stir 3 minutes. Pour into clean jars to within 1/2 inch of tops; wipe off rims of jars. Screw on lids. Allow jam to stand at room temperature 24 hours; store in freezer. Place in refrigerator 1 hour before serving. May be refrozen. Keeps up to 3 weeks in refrigerator or up to 1 year in freezer.

Yield: about 6 1/2 cups jam

Note: If making Peachy Jar Lids, store jam in wide-mouth canning jars.

PEACHY JAR LIDS

For each jar lid insert, you will need cream-colored paper; acetate for stencils (available at craft or art supply stores); craft knife; cutting mat or thick layer of newspapers; peach, coral, dark coral, green, and dark green acrylic paint; small stencil brushes; paper towels; brown permanent felt-tip pen with fine point; and removable tape (optional).

1. Referring to stencil cutting key and color key, follow Stenciling, page 122, to stencil peach on cream-colored paper.
2. Use brown pen to draw stem on peach.
3. Center ring of jar lid over stenciled peach and use a pencil to draw around outside of ring; cut out peach just inside drawn line.
4. Place insert in ring and screw in place over lid.

STENCIL CUTTING KEY
Stencil #1
Stencil #2

COLOR KEY
Stencil #1 (peach half) – peach shaded with dark coral
Stencil #1 (leaf half) – dark green
Stencil #2 (peach half) – coral shaded with dark coral
Stencil #2 (leaf half) – green

Zesty Hot Cheese Loaves

*O*ur Hot Garlic-Cheese Loaves are the perfect accompaniments to hearty winter entrées like soup, chili, or stew. Easily prepared with buttermilk baking mix, these mouth-watering loaves are perfect for taking along to potlucks or presenting to friends or coworkers. Pack them in a basket covered with a floral cross-stitched bread cloth for giving. The heartfelt sentiment is sure to brighten anyone's day.

HOT GARLIC-CHEESE LOAVES

3$^{1}/_{2}$	cups	buttermilk baking mix
2$^{1}/_{2}$	cups (10 ounces)	shredded sharp Cheddar cheese
1	teaspoon	garlic powder
$^{1}/_{4}$	teaspoon	ground red pepper
1$^{1}/_{4}$	cups	milk
2	eggs, beaten	

Preheat oven to 350 degrees. In a large bowl, combine baking mix, cheese, garlic powder, and red pepper. Add milk and eggs to dry ingredients; mix only until ingredients are moistened. Spoon batter into 4 greased and floured 3$^{1}/_{4}$ x 6-inch baking pans. Bake 30 to 35 minutes or until lightly browned. Cool in pans 5 minutes. Remove from pans and cool completely on a wire rack. Store in an airtight container.

Yield: 4 mini loaves bread

FLORAL BREAD CLOTH

You will need a white prefinished bread cover (14 ct) and embroidery floss (see color key).

Stitch design on 1 corner of bread cover, placing design 4 fabric threads from fringe. Use 2 strands of floss for Cross Stitch and 1 for Backstitch.

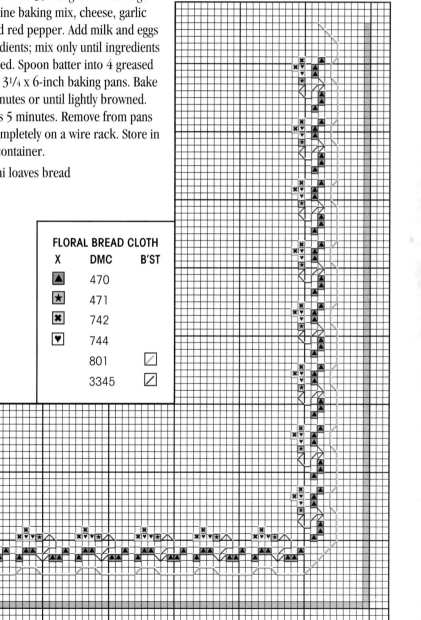

FLORAL BREAD CLOTH		
X	DMC	B'ST
▲	470	
★	471	
✖	742	
♥	744	
	801	◿
	3345	◿

VIVE LA FRENCH!

*S*alad lovers will rave *about our super-easy Creamy French Dressing! You can whip up this delicious concoction in a snap. Simply mix tomato soup and a handful of other ingredients and* voilà! — *a* pièce de résistance *that's perfect over salads or as a dip for fresh vegetables. Placed in a French canning jar topped with a decorative label, the sauce will make a wonderful gift when delivered in our muslin-lined basket. Add a coordinating Shaker box filled with purchased croutons, and you'll have an ideal way to wish your friend "Bon appétit!"*

CREAMY FRENCH DRESSING

$1/4$ cup pasteurized egg substitute
$1^1/2$ cups vegetable oil
1 cup salad dressing or mayonnaise
1 can ($10^3/4$ ounces) tomato soup, undiluted
$1/2$ cup tarragon vinegar
1 teaspoon garlic powder
$1/2$ teaspoon salt

In a medium bowl, beat egg substitute with an electric mixer until foamy. Continue beating while slowly adding oil, then salad dressing; beat until well blended. Add remaining ingredients; beat until smooth. Store in an airtight container in refrigerator. Serve with salads or use as a dip for fresh vegetables.

Yield: about 4 cups dressing

SALAD SET

You will need a basket, jar, Shaker box, muslin, $1^1/2$"w craft ribbon, $3/4$"w paper-backed fusible web tape, cream-colored paper, clear self-adhesive plastic (Con-tact® paper), black felt-tip pen with fine point, a colored pencil, three 21" lengths of $1/16$"w satin ribbon, craft glue, and a hole punch.

1. For basket liner, cut a square of muslin desired size. Cut 4 lengths of craft ribbon and 8 lengths of web tape the same length as 1 edge of muslin square.
2. With wrong sides together, press each length of craft ribbon in half lengthwise.
3. Follow manufacturer's instructions to fuse 1 length of web tape along 1 edge of muslin. Do not remove paper backing. Turn muslin over and fuse a second web length along same edge. Remove paper backing from both lengths. Insert webbed edge of muslin into fold of 1 ribbon length; fuse in place. Repeat for remaining edges of liner. Place liner in basket.
4. For jar lid label, use top of lid as a pattern to cut a circle from cream-colored paper. Trim circle to fit top of lid. Use pen to draw design around edge of label and to write "Creamy French Dressing" on label. Use colored pencil to color edge of label. Cut a piece of self-adhesive plastic slightly larger than label. Apply plastic to right side of label; trim plastic even with edge of label. Glue label to top of lid.
5. For Shaker box label, cut a label from paper smaller than lid. Use pen to draw design around edge of label and to write "Croutons" on label. Use colored pencil to color edge of label. Glue label to center of lid. Use top of lid as pattern to cut a piece of self-adhesive plastic. Apply plastic to lid.
6. Measure around side of Shaker box; add $1/2$". Cut a length of craft ribbon the determined measurement. Glue ribbon around box.
7. For tag, cut a $2^1/2$" x $3^1/2$" piece of paper. Matching short edges, fold paper in half. Use pen to draw a line $3/8$" from edges of tag and to write "Pour Vous" on tag. Use colored pencil to color edge of tag. Punch a hole in tag. Use satin ribbon lengths to tie tag to basket.

CINCO DE MAYO SANGRIA

*O*n May 5, celebrate Mexico's Cinco de Mayo festivities with a gift of fruity, refreshing Sangria! Our flavorful version of this favorite South-of-the-Border beverage blends juices, drink mixes, and red wine or grape juice for a spirited cooler that's sure to please. Presented in a colorful, simple-to-make fabric bag, your gift will be muy bueno!

SANGRIA

- 1 can (46 ounces) pineapple juice, chilled
- 1 quart orange juice, chilled
- 1 package (0.13 ounces) unsweetened raspberry-flavored soft drink mix
- 1 package (0.13 ounces) unsweetened cherry-flavored soft drink mix
- 2 cups sugar
- 4 cups water
- 1 liter red wine *or* 1 quart grape juice, chilled

    Fresh orange slices and maraschino cherries to garnish

In a 1¹/₂-gallon container, combine pineapple and orange juices, drink mixes, and sugar; stir until well blended and sugar is dissolved. Add water and wine or grape juice. Cover and store in refrigerator. Garnish individual drinks or punch bowl with fresh orange slices and maraschino cherries.

Yield: about twenty-four 6-ounce servings

FABRIC BAG AND GIFT TAG

You will need fabric for bag, thread to match fabric, 12" of braid trim, 5" of jute twine, a 2³/₄" square of cream-colored paper, a 3¹/₂" square of colored heavy paper, black felt-tip pen with medium point, craft glue, and a hole punch.

1. For bag, follow Fabric Bag instructions, page 122.

2. Place container of Sangria in bag. Knot braid trim around top of bag.

3. For tag, glue cream-colored paper square to heavy paper square. Use pen to write "Cinco de Mayo" on tag. Punch a hole in tag. Use twine to tie tag to braid trim on bag.

GRILL OUT!

A *friend who enjoys cooking out will savor a gift of our aromatic Grilled Meat Seasoning. Flavorful spices, blended with brown sugar, enhance the natural goodness of pork or poultry. A handy oven mitt with a bold "Grill Out!" tag is a nice way to round out your gift.*

GRILLED MEAT SEASONING

$1/2$ cup firmly packed brown sugar
  2 tablespoons ground cumin seed
  2 tablespoons chili powder
  1 teaspoon ground cinnamon
  1 teaspoon ground nutmeg
  1 teaspoon garlic powder
  1 teaspoon onion powder
  1 teaspoon salt
$1/2$ teaspoon ground red pepper
$1/2$ teaspoon ground black pepper

In a small bowl, combine all ingredients until well blended. Store in an airtight container. Give with serving instructions.

Yield: about $1 1/4$ cups seasoning

To serve: Generously sprinkle seasoning on raw meat about 2 hours before cooking; return meat to refrigerator to allow flavors to be absorbed. Grill or broil as desired. Especially good with pork and poultry.

For mitt, tie a length of $7/8$"w grosgrain ribbon around a purchased mitt. For tag, cut a $2 1/2$" dia. circle from white paper and a $2 3/4$" dia. circle from heavy black paper. Use a black felt-tip pen with fine point and a ruler to draw grid lines $1/4$" apart on white circle. Use craft glue to glue white circle to center of black circle. Use a red felt-tip pen with broad point to write "Grill Out!" on tag. Punch a hole in top of tag. Use a length of $1/8$"w satin ribbon to tie tag to ribbon on mitt.

BUTTERSCOTCH COFFEE CAKE

*E*asily created with a package of frozen rolls, this Butterscotch Coffee Cake is a delicious way to extend warm wishes. The sweet cinnamon-spiced topping, enhanced with pecans and butterscotch pudding mix, is sure to please! Take the cake over to a neighbor's house straight from the oven for a treat that's melt-in-your-mouth wonderful.

BUTTERSCOTCH COFFEE CAKE

- 1 package (25 ounces) frozen white dinner rolls
- ¹/₂ cup sugar
- 1 package (3.5 ounces) butterscotch pudding and pie filling mix
- 1 tablespoon ground cinnamon
- ¹/₂ cup butter or margarine, melted
- 1 cup chopped pecans

Place frozen rolls in bottom of a greased 12-cup fluted tube pan. In a small bowl, combine sugar, pudding mix, and cinnamon. Sprinkle sugar mixture over rolls. Pour butter over sugar mixture. Sprinkle pecans on top. Cover with plastic wrap and let rise in a warm place (80 to 85 degrees) 5¹/₂ to 6¹/₂ hours or until doubled in size. To serve in early morning, coffee cake can rise overnight (about 8 hours).

Preheat oven to 350 degrees. Bake 30 to 35 minutes or until golden brown. Remove from oven and immediately invert onto plate. Serve warm.

Yield: about 16 servings

"PEACHY KEEN" SAUCE

*T*reat your friends to "peachy keen" delicacy with our Peach Melba Sauce. Served over ice cream or other desserts, this tangy mixture of peach and raspberry preserves and red currant jelly has just a hint of peach brandy. Present your offering in a jar topped with a pretty gathered paper napkin for a peach of a gift.

PEACH MELBA SAUCE

2 jars (12 ounces each) peach
     preserves
2 jars (12 ounces each) raspberry
     preserves
2 jars (12 ounces each) red currant
     jelly
3 tablespoons peach brandy

In a large saucepan, combine preserves and jelly over medium-high heat. Stirring occasionally, heat preserve mixture until melted and well blended; remove from heat. Stir in brandy. Store in an airtight container in refrigerator. Serve warm or cold with ice cream, fruit, pudding, muffins, or cake.

Yield: about 6¹/₂ cups sauce

For gathered napkin jar topper, unfold a 10" paper napkin. At center of wrong side of napkin, gather a ¹/₂" long section of napkin; wrap a rubber band tightly around gathered section. Center napkin right side up on jar lid. Wrap a rubber band around napkin to secure napkin to jar. Tie three 26" lengths of satin ribbon into a bow around napkin, covering rubber band.

BREAKFAST BUTTERS

Our sweetly flavored butters will start the day off right! With varieties like Strawberry, Almond-Peach, Cinnamon-Maple, and Honey-Orange, they're sure to please. Each whips up in an instant and keeps in the refrigerator until you're ready to surprise your friends. For gift-giving, glue fabric to paper bags and glue on heart-shaped labels.

FLAVORED BUTTERS

ALMOND-PEACH BUTTER

$1/2$ cup butter, softened
$1/3$ cup peach preserves
$1/2$ teaspoon almond extract
$1/2$ teaspoon confectioners sugar

HONEY-ORANGE BUTTER

$1/2$ cup butter, softened
$1/4$ cup honey
2 tablespoons orange marmalade

CINNAMON-MAPLE BUTTER

$1/2$ cup butter, softened
2 tablespoons maple syrup
$1/2$ teaspoon ground cinnamon

STRAWBERRY BUTTER

$1/2$ cup butter, softened
$1/3$ cup strawberry preserves
$1/2$ teaspoon lemon juice
$1/2$ teaspoon confectioners sugar

For each flavor of butter, whip butter with electric mixer in a small bowl until smooth and fluffy; gradually add remaining ingredients. Store in an airtight container in refrigerator.

Yield: four flavored butters about $3/4$ to 1 cup each

BUTTER BAGS

For each bag, you will need a $4^{1}/_{4}$" x $7^{3}/_{4}$" paper bag, a 5" x $8^{1}/_{2}$" fabric piece, cream-colored paper, 12" of cotton string, brown and red felt-tip pens with fine points, paper-backed fusible web, craft glue, tracing paper, and a $1/8$" hole punch.

1. Follow manufacturer's instructions to fuse web to wrong side of fabric. Cut a piece from fabric slightly smaller than front of bag. Remove paper backing. With 1 short edge of fabric even with top edge of bag, center and fuse fabric to front of bag.
2. For heart, trace heart pattern, page 118, onto tracing paper; cut out. Use pattern to cut heart from cream-colored paper. Use brown pen to draw dashed lines along edge of heart to resemble stitches. Use red pen to write butter flavor on heart. Glue heart to front of bag.
3. Place jar of butter in bag.
4. Fold top of bag $1^{1}/_{4}$" to front. Punch two holes in bag $1/2$" apart near top fold of bag. Thread string through holes and tie into a bow at front of bag.

WESTERN ROUNDUP

*Y*ou'll round up lots of compliments with this Western-style gift! It'll only take a few minutes to rustle up the fixin's for Cheesy Black-Eyed Pea Dip — and you'll have plenty to share with your favorite cowpokes. Tied with a raffia-laced concha, a classic red cowboy bandanna makes a unique topper for a jar of the dip. Pack the spicy snack in a brown paper bag and add crispy tortilla chips, and your saddle pals will holler "Yee-ha!"

CHEESY BLACK-EYED PEA DIP

- 3 cans (16 ounces each) black-eyed peas, drained
- 2 cups (8 ounces) shredded sharp Cheddar cheese
- 1 can (4 ounces) chopped green chilies, drained
- 1/2 cup butter or margarine, cut into pieces
- 2 tablespoons dried chopped onion
- 1 1/2 tablespoons diced jalapeño peppers
- 1/4 teaspoon garlic powder

In a large microwave-safe bowl, combine all ingredients. Microwave on medium-high power (80%) 6 minutes, stirring every 2 minutes. Store in an airtight container in refrigerator. Serve warm with chips.

Yield: about 5 cups dip

For bandanna jar topper, fold a 21" square bandanna in half from top to bottom and again from right to left. Center bandanna over jar lid. Wrap a rubber band around bandanna to secure bandanna to jar. Tie raffia around bandanna, covering rubber band. Thread ends of raffia through concha and tie again.

BERRY PATCH BREAD

Like friendships, berries need warmth to grow to their sweet splendor. Your friends will taste the sunshine in every bite of our moist and fruity Strawberry Bread. It's surprisingly easy to make with dry biscuit mix and frozen fruit! Delivered in a cheery basket dressed up with a berry-print cloth and a bright gingham bow, your gift will be remembered long after the bread is gone.

STRAWBERRY BREAD

- 3 cups buttermilk biscuit mix
- 1/2 cup granulated sugar
- 1 package (3 ounces) strawberry-flavored gelatin
- 1 teaspoon dried lemon peel
- 2 packages (10 ounces each) frozen sliced strawberries, thawed and divided
- 3 eggs
- 1 cup sifted confectioners sugar

Preheat oven to 350 degrees. In a large bowl, combine biscuit mix, granulated sugar, gelatin, and lemon peel. Reserving 3/4 cup liquid, drain strawberries. Add 1 cup strawberries, 1/2 cup reserved strawberry liquid, and eggs to dry ingredients. Beat at low speed of an electric mixer 30 seconds; increase to high speed and beat 3 minutes longer. Spoon batter into 2 greased and floured 4 x 8-inch loaf pans. Bake 50 to 55 minutes or until a toothpick inserted in center comes out clean. Cool in pans 10 minutes. Remove from pans and transfer to a wire rack with waxed paper underneath.

For glaze, combine confectioners sugar, 1/4 cup reserved strawberry liquid, and remaining strawberries in a small bowl; beat until smooth. Drizzle glaze over warm bread. Allow glaze to harden. Store in an airtight container.

Yield: 2 loaves bread

For basket liner, follow Easy Basket Liner instructions, page 122.

FRIENDSHIP COFFEE MIX

Mocha-Nut Coffee Mix

*S*pecial friends deserve
special treats, and yours will
be delighted with this pretty
gift of good taste. Our
gourmet Mocha-Nut Coffee
Mix makes a rich, soothing
beverage that's perfect
anytime — day or night.
Package the mix in a flower-
rimmed bag and give with a
delicate mug cross stitched in
lovely shades of lavender,
blue, and green. What a
super gift idea for a birthday,
Friendship Day, or any day
you want to show someone
how much you care.

MOCHA-NUT COFFEE MIX

1 can (30 ounces) instant hot
    cocoa mix
1¼ cups instant coffee granules
2½ teaspoons vanilla butter and
    nut extract

In a medium bowl, combine all
ingredients until well blended. Store in
an airtight container. Give with serving
instructions.

Yield: about 6 cups coffee mix

To serve: Stir 3 rounded teaspoons coffee
mix into 6 ounces hot water.

CROSS-STITCHED MUG

You will need a Stitch-A-Mug™ with Vinyl-
Weave® (14 ct) insert and embroidery floss
(see color key).

Beginning 3 stitches from left short edge,
center and stitch design on insert using 3
strands of floss for Cross Stitch and 2 for
Backstitch. Repeat design to 2 stitches from
right short edge. Place stitched piece in
mug with short edges of vinyl aligned with
handle.

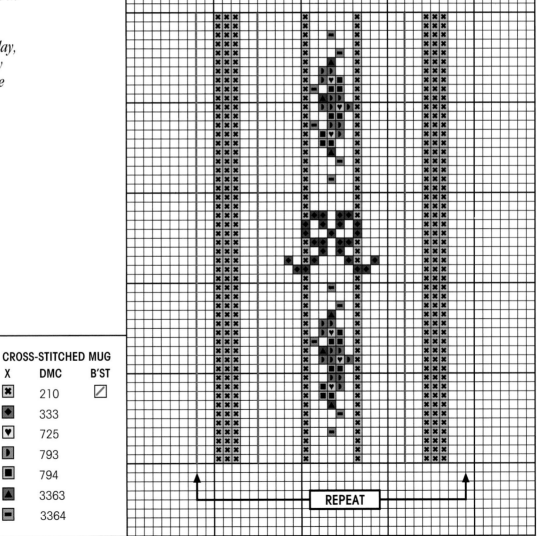

CROSS-STITCHED MUG

X	DMC	B'ST
✶	210	⧄
◆	333	
♥	725	
◗	793	
■	794	
▲	3363	
▬	3364	

REPEAT

"Beary" Good Cookies

BEAR BASKET

Lift someone's spirits with a big bear hug and our basket of irresistible Chocolate-Oatmeal-Raisin Cookies! Ever so simple to prepare, they begin with pound cake mix and contain a sweet surprise — chocolate-covered raisins! Clever cutouts of overall-clad bears surround the basket to help express your "beary" best wishes for a wonderful day.

You will need a basket with handle, brown craft paper, fabric for overalls, fabric to line basket, paper-backed fusible web, brown and pink colored pencils, cream-colored paper, tracing paper, transparent tape, removable tape, hot glue gun, and glue sticks.

1. Trace bear and overalls patterns onto tracing paper; cut out.
2. For bears, measure around basket rim; add 3". Using transparent tape to piece paper as necessary, cut a 5"w strip of craft paper the determined measurement.
3. Spacing folds 3" apart, fanfold paper strip. Use removable tape to tape edges of paper together so paper will not shift when cutting.
4. With dotted lines of pattern along folds of paper, center bear pattern on folded paper;

draw around pattern. Cut out bear along solid lines only. Unfold paper strip and cut off any partial bears.
5. For overalls, follow manufacturer's instructions to fuse web to wrong side of overalls fabric. Use overalls pattern to cut 1 pair of overalls from fabric for each bear. Fuse overalls to bears.
6. Use brown pencil to draw eyes, nose, mouth, and ears on each bear. Use pink pencil to draw cheeks.
7. Centering 1 bear below basket handle, glue bears around rim of basket.
8. For signs, cut three 1" x 2⅝" pieces from cream-colored paper. Use brown pencil to write "chocolate," "oatmeal," and "raisin" on signs. Glue signs to bears.
9. Line basket with fabric.

CHOCOLATE-OATMEAL-RAISIN COOKIES

1	package (16 ounces) pound cake mix
¾	cup vegetable oil
2	eggs
1	teaspoon vanilla extract
½	teaspoon ground cinnamon
1	cup quick-cooking oats
¾	cup (about 6 ounces) chocolate-covered raisins

Preheat oven to 375 degrees. In a large bowl, combine cake mix, oil, eggs, vanilla, and cinnamon; beat with an electric mixer until smooth. Stir in oats and raisins. Drop tablespoonfuls of dough about 2 inches apart on an ungreased baking sheet. Bake 8 to 10 minutes or until edges are light brown. Transfer to a wire rack to cool completely. Store in an airtight container.

Yield: about 4 dozen cookies

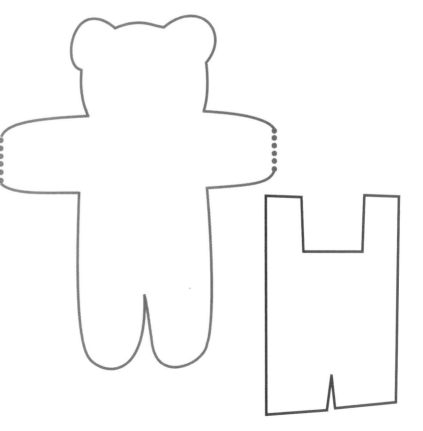

EASY CORN CASSEROLE

*F*or a dish that's really hot-to-go, give this savory Mexican Corn Casserole. Green chilies add pizzazz to the mingling flavors of sweet corn and Cheddar cheese. It's extra-easy to make with corn muffin mix and canned corn, and the recipe makes two delicious casseroles. Presented with colorful painted pot holders, this South-of-the-Border delight will have everyone shouting "Olé!"

MEXICAN CORN CASSEROLES

- 2 cans (11 ounces each) Mexican-style corn, drained
- 1 can (16¹/₂ ounces) yellow cream-style corn
- 1 package (8.5 ounces) corn muffin mix
- 1 cup (4 ounces) shredded sharp Cheddar cheese
- ¹/₂ cup sour cream
- 1 can (4 ounces) chopped green chilies, drained
- ¹/₄ cup butter or margarine, melted

Preheat oven to 350 degrees. Stir all ingredients in a large bowl until just combined. Pour batter into 2 greased 9-inch iron skillets or two 8-inch square baking pans. Bake 45 to 55 minutes or until lightly browned. Cover and store in refrigerator. Give with serving instructions.

Yield: 2 casseroles, about 8 servings each

To serve: Cover and bake in a preheated 350-degree oven 20 to 25 minutes or until heated through.

For painted pot holders, use fabric paint to paint within machine-stitched quilting lines on a purchased pot holder.

HAPPY HOUR BASKET

*S*how a favorite couple how much they mean to you with a gift basket containing our creamy Herb Cheese Spread and some savory crackers. By simply blending cream cheese, butter, and half a dozen herbs and spices, you can make the spread in minutes! Add a clever tag and individual bottles of wine, and you'll help their cocktail hour get off to a lively start.

HERB CHEESE SPREAD

  1 package (8 ounces) cream cheese, softened
 1/4 cup butter or margarine, softened
1 1/2 tablespoons milk
 1/4 teaspoon garlic powder
 1/4 teaspoon ground savory
 1/8 teaspoon ground oregano
 1/8 teaspoon dried dill weed
 1/8 teaspoon dried basil leaves
 1/8 teaspoon ground black pepper

In a small bowl, beat all ingredients with an electric mixer until well blended. Store in an airtight container in refrigerator. Serve with crackers or over hot pasta or vegetables.

Yield: about 1 1/3 cups spread

For tag, use craft glue to glue a 3" x 4" piece of poster board to center of wrong side of a 6" x 8" piece of glossy wrapping paper. Fold and glue edges of paper to back of poster board. Glue 1 end each of two 3" lengths of 3/4"w glossy ribbon to back of tag; trim remaining ends diagonally. Use dimensional paint to write "Happy Hour" at center of tag; before paint dries, apply glitter to paint. Allow to dry; shake off excess glitter. Use dimensional paint to paint dots on tag and "for 2!" on ribbons; allow to dry. Form several 10" lengths of satin ribbon into a double-loop bow; tie another length around center to secure. Glue bow to tag.

TROPICAL CRUNCH

*G*ive a friend a taste of the tropics with our Tropical Crunch Snack Mix. With only five ingredients to toss together, you can mix up lots of this delicious, all-natural treat in a minute (or less)! For a sunny presentation, line a child's plastic pail with cellophane and include a plastic toy shovel for serving. So clever, so cute, and so "munch" fun to eat!

TROPICAL CRUNCH SNACK MIX

- 1 can (12 ounces) honey-roasted peanuts
- 1 can (10 ounces) salted cashews
- 10 ounces dried banana chips
- 8 ounces dried pineapple pieces
- 6 ounces coconut chips

Combine all ingredients in a large bowl. Store in an airtight container.

Yield: about 11 cups snack mix

BLUEBERRY-ORANGE VINEGAR

*O*ur zesty Blueberry-Orange Vinegar makes it easy to add a burst of flavor to any meal. Lightly sweetened with honey, the tangy condiment is perfect for sprinkling on fruit, meat, or tossed salad — or it can be substituted in recipes for extra zip. To share with friends, pour the fruity vinegar into bottles and add handwritten labels and tags made from rag paper.

BLUEBERRY-ORANGE VINEGAR

- 1 quart white wine vinegar
- 1/4 cup honey
- 1 cup frozen whole blueberries
- 6 4-inch strips orange zest

In a 2-quart measuring cup with spout, combine vinegar and honey; stir until well blended. Divide orange zest and blueberries evenly into desired number of gift containers. Pour vinegar mixture into containers. Allow vinegar to stand for 1 week to allow flavors to blend. Serve over fruit salad, meat salad, or salad greens.

Yield: about 5 cups vinegar

BOTTLE LABEL AND TAG

You will need taupe and cream-colored handmade paper (available at art supply stores), artificial blueberries and leaves, 1 dried orange wedge, gold paint pen with fine point, black felt-tip pens with medium and fine points, hot glue gun, glue sticks, a hole punch, and jute twine.

1. For label, cut a 3" x 4" piece from taupe paper. Use paint pen to paint a line 3/4" from edges of label. Use black pen with medium point to write "Blueberry-Orange Vinegar" on label. Glue label to bottle. Glue leaves, blueberries, and orange wedge to label.

2. For tag, tear a 2³/₄" square from cream-colored paper. Cut a 2" square from taupe paper. Glue small square to center of large square. Use paint pen to paint a line just outside small square. Use black pen with medium point to write "To:" and "From:" on tag. Use black pen with fine point to write names on tag. Punch a hole in tag. Tie a length of twine around bottle; thread ends through tag and tie into a bow.

CHOCOLATE LOVER'S SAUCE

*D*elight any chocolate lover with a gift of luscious Orange-Chocolate Sauce. Drizzled over cake or ice cream, it transforms an ordinary dessert into a spectacular treat! It's easily prepared with ingredients commonly kept in your kitchen. To present, simply fill a jar with the tasty topping and place it in a basket adorned with a dried orange slice and craft ribbon. "Orange" you sweet to remember special friends!

ORANGE-CHOCOLATE SAUCE

- 1 can (12 ounces) evaporated milk
- 1 package (6 ounces) semisweet chocolate chips
- ½ cup butter or margarine
- ½ cup frozen orange juice concentrate, thawed
- 2 cups sifted confectioners sugar
- 1 teaspoon orange extract

In a medium saucepan, combine milk, chocolate chips, butter, and orange juice concentrate. Stirring constantly, cook over low heat until smooth. Increase heat to medium-high. Gradually stir in confectioners sugar and bring to a boil. Stirring constantly, reduce heat to medium-low and boil 8 minutes. Remove from heat; stir in orange extract. Cool to room temperature. Store in an airtight container in refrigerator. Serve warm or cold with ice cream or cake.

Yield: about 3 cups sauce

A TOASTY TREAT

*I*t's easy to give your "sugar" a special breakfast treat with our Vanilla-cinnamon Sugar! Sweet and spicy, the sugar adds a flavorful twist to cinnamon toast, and it's great with cereal and fresh fruit, too. For a toasty surprise, tuck a jar of the sugar in a fabric-lined basket. Realistic-looking "toast" slices made from sponges add a bit of fun to kitchen cleanup.

VANILLA-CINNAMON SUGAR

   4 cups sugar
 1/4 cup ground cinnamon
   1 whole vanilla bean, cut into
          1-inch pieces

In a medium bowl, combine all ingredients. Store in an airtight container for two weeks to allow flavors to blend. Remove vanilla bean pieces. Sprinkle sugar on toast, unbaked cookies, cereal, fruit, or stir into drinks. Flavored sugar may be substituted for granulated sugar in baking.

Yield: about 4 cups sugar

TOASTY BASKET

You will need a basket; fabric square for liner; satin ribbons; cream-colored paper; 2 white Miracle Sponges™; tracing paper; brown permanent felt-tip pens with fine and broad points; brown, yellow, and orange colored pencils; and a 1/8" hole punch.

1. Fringe edges of fabric square 1/4" and place in basket.
2. For bread slices, trace large bread slice pattern, page 119, onto tracing paper; cut out. Use pattern to cut 1 slice from each sponge. Wet slices and allow to dry. Use pen with broad point to color edge of each slice to resemble crust.

3. For tag, trace small bread slice pattern, page 119, onto tracing paper; cut out. Use pattern to cut 1 slice from cream-colored paper. Use pen with fine point to write "GOOD MORNING, SUGAR" on tag. Use orange and yellow colored pencils to highlight "SUGAR." Use brown and yellow colored pencils to color tag to resemble bread slice. Punch a hole at top of tag. Tie ribbons around top of sugar container. Thread tag onto ribbons; tie ribbons into a bow.

PEOPLE CHOW

*Y*our family and friends will howl with delight when they sink their teeth into this sweet, crunchy snack. Offer People Chow to a special friend who's been in the "doghouse," or to anybody who needs a little cheering up. Easy to make by coating cereal with a chocolate-peanut butter mixture, this mouth-watering snack is sure to make everyone sit up and beg for more! Packaged in cellophane and tied with a satin ribbon, the zany gift is complete when presented in a brand new doggie dish with a whimsical doghouse name tag!

PEOPLE CHOW

- 1 package (6 ounces) chocolate chips
- 1/2 cup butter or margarine
- 1/2 cup creamy peanut butter
- 1/2 teaspoon ground cinnamon
- 8 cups round toasted oat cereal
- 2 to 3 cups sifted confectioners sugar

Stirring constantly, melt chocolate chips and butter in a medium saucepan over medium heat. Remove from heat. Add peanut butter and cinnamon; stir until smooth. Place cereal in a large bowl. Pour chocolate mixture over cereal; stir until evenly coated. Pour confectioners sugar into a large paper bag; add chocolate-coated cereal. Gently shake bag until mixture is evenly coated with sugar. Spread onto waxed paper; allow to cool completely. Store in an airtight container.

Yield: about 13 cups snack mix

For tag, trace patterns, page 119, onto tracing paper; cut out. Use patterns to cut doghouse from white paper and roof from blue paper. Use a brown colored pencil to color doghouse. Use craft glue to glue doghouse to a piece of black paper. Leaving black paper in door opening, cut black paper even with edges of doghouse. With top edge of roof even with top edge of doghouse, glue roof to doghouse. For name cut a 1/2" x 13/4" strip of white paper. Use a black felt-tip pen with fine point to write name and draw paw prints on strip. Glue strip to doghouse.

ONION DIP DELIGHT

*S*ummer is an ideal time to share this garden-fresh dip. Enhanced with a hint of dill, our Vidalia Onion Dip is as easy as pie to make! Simply blend together fresh onions and Parmesan cheese with a handful of other ingredients, bake until lightly browned, and refrigerate until ready to give. Then wrap the dish in cellophane, trim with a silk wildflower and a raffia bow, and add the serving instructions. What a great way to enjoy the summer abundance of sweet Vidalia onions!

VIDALIA ONION DIP

    2 large Vidalia or other mild onions,
          quartered
1¹/₂ cups freshly shredded
          Parmesan cheese, divided
    1 cup mayonnaise
    1 cup sour cream
2¹/₂ teaspoons dried dill weed,
          divided

Preheat oven to 325 degrees. In a food processor, process onions until finely chopped. Add 1 cup cheese, mayonnaise, sour cream, and 2 teaspoons dill weed; process until well blended. Spoon mixture into two 9-inch glass pie plates. Sprinkle tops evenly with remaining ¹/₂ cup cheese and remaining ¹/₂ teaspoon dill weed. Bake 40 to 45 minutes or until lightly browned. Store in an airtight container in refrigerator. Give with serving instructions.

Yield: about 4 cups dip

To serve: Serve with chips or crackers at room temperature or reheat in a microwave-safe container in microwave on medium-high power (80%) about 3 minutes or until heated through.

A NUTTY TREAT

*Y*our friends and family will go nuts for these delicious Peanut Butter-Fudge Cookies. Whipped up with chunky peanut butter and a package of fudge brownie mix, the chewy morsels make quick gifts. Pile them in a basket and add our peanut gift tag, and the person you're nuts about is sure to get the message.

PEANUT BUTTER-FUDGE COOKIES

  1 cup chunky peanut butter
  2 tablespoons vegetable oil
  2 eggs
  1 package (21.5 ounces) fudge brownie mix
  1/2 cup water
  1 package (6 ounces) semisweet chocolate chips
  1 cup chopped unsalted peanuts

Preheat oven to 350 degrees. In a large bowl, beat peanut butter, oil, and eggs. Add brownie mix and water; stir until moistened. Stir in chocolate chips. Drop tablespoonfuls of dough onto an ungreased baking sheet. Place 1/2 teaspoon peanuts on each cookie. Bake 12 to 14 minutes or until fingertip leaves a slight indentation when center of cookie is touched. Transfer to a wire rack to cool completely. Store in an airtight container.

Yield: about 5 dozen cookies

For tag, trace peanut pattern onto tracing paper; cut out. Use pattern to cut peanut from brown craft paper. Use spray adhesive to glue peanut to black paper. Trim black paper to 1/8" from peanut. Use brown felt-tip pen with fine point to draw detail lines on peanut. Use brown felt-tip pen with broad point to write "Nuts about you!" on peanut. Use black felt-tip pen with fine point to write over letters. Use a 1/8" hole punch to punch hole at top of tag. Use jute to tie tag to basket.

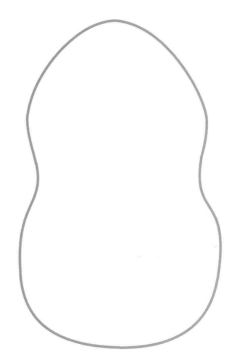

BANANA SPLIT SAUCE

A perfect topping for ice cream, this delectable Banana Split Sauce is an "a-peeling" way to satisfy a dessert lover! The chocolaty syrup is brimming with dried banana chips, chopped pecans, and cherries. It's easy to mix up, and the recipe yields enough for several gifts. To present, tuck a jar of the sauce and some sundae glasses in a pretty fabric-lined basket. Adorned with a Neapolitan-style bow and a banana tag, it's the sweetest offering you could ever give!

BANANA SPLIT SAUCE

- 1 jar (18 ounces) cherry preserves
- 1 container (48 ounces) chocolate-flavored syrup
- 1 cup coarsely chopped pecans, toasted
- 1 cup dried banana chips
- 1 jar (6 ounces) maraschino cherries, drained and coarsely chopped

In a large microwave-safe bowl, microwave preserves on medium-high power (80%) 4 to 5 minutes or until melted. Stir in remaining ingredients. Store in an airtight container in refrigerator. Serve warm or cold with ice cream or cake.

Yield: about 7 cups sauce

For tag, trace banana pattern, page 120, onto tracing paper; cut out. Use pattern to cut banana from a piece of heavy yellow paper. Use dark yellow, green, brown, and dark brown colored pencils to color banana. Use brown pencil to write "BANANA SPLIT SAUCE" on tag. Use a 1/8" hole punch to punch a hole at top of tag. Use white satin cord to tie tag to basket handle.

PRETTY PRETZEL TREATS

*M*ake any occasion extra special with a gift of elegant Raspberry-Chocolate Pretzel Treats. Deliciously easy to create, the pretzels are simply dipped in a chocolaty candy coating and drizzled with tinted raspberry-flavored icing. For an eye-catching delivery, package your offering in a pretty jar tied with a colorful ribbon. A handmade tag adds a delightful finishing touch.

RASPBERRY-CHOCOLATE PRETZEL TREATS

- 14 ounces chocolate-flavored candy coating
- 1 package (10 ounces) 2½-inch-wide pretzel knots
- 1 cup sifted confectioners sugar
- 2 tablespoons milk
- 4 drops raspberry-flavored oil Burgundy paste food coloring

In a heavy medium saucepan, melt candy coating over low heat, stirring frequently. Using a large fork or dipping fork, dip pretzels into chocolate. Transfer to a baking sheet covered with waxed paper. Place in refrigerator to allow coating to harden.

For icing, mix confectioners sugar, milk, and raspberry-flavored oil in a small bowl until smooth. If necessary, icing may be thinned by adding additional milk 1 teaspoon at a time. Divide icing evenly into 2 small bowls. Tint 1 bowl light pink and one bowl dark pink. Place pretzels on a wire rack with waxed paper underneath. Drizzle both colors of icing over pretzels. Allow icing to harden. Store in an airtight container.

Yield: about 25 pretzels

For tag, follow manufacturer's instructions to fuse paper-backed fusible web to wrong sides of pink and green fabrics. Cut 3 approx. ½" dia. circles and 2 approx. 1" long leaf shapes from fabrics. Remove paper backing. Fuse leaves and berries to a 3" x 3¾" piece of heavy paper. Use brown felt-tip pen to draw stems on paper. Use pink felt-tip pen to write "raspberry-chocolate pretzel treats" on tag. Punch a hole in tag; thread tag onto ribbon.

A SPARKLING SALUTE

*W*hat a sweet surprise! Sure to liven up a New Year's Eve party, this top hat is overflowing with merriment. We've blended together some frozen juice concentrates to make a colorful, fruity base. Your friends have the option of adding sparkling grape juice or wine to ensure that the New Year gets off to a really spirited beginning. You'll want to mix up both versions so all revelers can enjoy the late-night festivities.

SPARKLING FRUIT PUNCH

1 can (12 ounces) frozen apple-grape-raspberry juice concentrate, thawed

1 can (6 ounces) frozen lemonade concentrate, thawed

1 bottle (25 ounces) sparkling red grape juice *or* 1 fifth (750 ml) sparkling wine, chilled

Combine frozen juice concentrates in a 1-quart container. Cover and store in refrigerator. Give with serving instructions.

Yield: about seven 6-ounce servings

To serve: Combine blended concentrates and sparkling grape juice or wine. Serve chilled.

FROSTY CONFECTION

*H*elp a friend start
the new year off right! Our
Almond Tortoni is an Italian-
style frozen dessert created
with lightly sweetened
whipped cream mixed with
almonds and almond liqueur.
The luscious confection is
garnished with nuts and
cherries and presented in a
ribbon-tied take-out box.
Colorful confetti glued
around the edges of the gift
bag adds a sparkly touch.

ALMOND TORTONI

  2   cups whipping cream
¼   cup sifted confectioners sugar
¼   cup amaretto
½   cup finely ground almonds,
        toasted

      Toasted sliced almonds and
          maraschino cherries with stems
          to garnish

   Place a medium bowl and beaters from
an electric mixer in freezer until well
chilled. In chilled bowl, whip cream
until soft peaks form. Gradually add
confectioners sugar and amaretto; beat until
stiff peaks form. Fold in ground almonds.
Spoon mixture into 12 paper-lined muffin
tins. Garnish with almond slices and
cherries. Freeze until firm; cover. Remove
from freezer about 15 minutes before
serving.

Yield: 12 servings

A Bit Of Elegance

*T*reat your friends to a little luxury on Valentine's Day with richly flavored Almond-Brandy Truffles. Everyone will think they came from a gourmet candy shop! Our simple recipe makes enough for several gifts, so you can share with all your special friends. And no one will guess that the beautiful pins atop the gift boxes were easily crafted using wrapping paper motifs, dried flowers, and heart-shaped charms.

ALMOND-BRANDY TRUFFLES

2/3 cup whipping cream
6 ounces unsweetened baking
   chocolate, finely chopped
1/2 cup sifted confectioners sugar
1/4 cup almond paste
3 tablespoons brandy
1 cup finely ground almonds, toasted

In a small saucepan, bring cream to a boil over medium-low heat. Remove from heat; add chocolate and stir until melted. Combine chocolate mixture, confectioners sugar, almond paste, and brandy in a medium bowl. Spread mixture in an 8-inch square glass baking dish. Cover and refrigerate 1 hour or until firm enough to shape.

Using a melon baller or small spoon, shape into 1-inch balls; roll in ground almonds. Store in an airtight container in refrigerator.

Yield: about 3 dozen truffles

SWEETHEART PINS

For each pin, you will need wrapping paper with desired motif, paper-backed fusible web, tagboard (manila folder), Clear Clear Cote (a clear gloss finish for paper crafts available at craft stores), dried miniature rosebuds and greenery, pearl beads, a heart-shaped charm, small bow tied from 1/4"w satin ribbon (optional), small acrylic jewel (optional), pin back, hot glue gun, and glue sticks.

1. Cutting 1" outside of motif, cut motif from wrapping paper. Cut a piece of web slightly smaller than wrapping paper. Follow manufacturer's instructions to fuse web to wrong side of wrapping paper. Fuse wrapping paper to tagboard. Cut out motif.
2. Use a 1/4" x 3" strip of tagboard to apply a thick coat of Clear Clear Cote to motif, being sure to bring coating to edges. Lay motif flat and allow to dry 1 to 2 days.
3. Hot glue rosebuds, greenery, pearl beads, and charm to motif. If desired, hot glue bow and jewel to motif. Hot glue pin back to back of motif.

SWEETHEART FUDGE

*O*ne bite of our Peanut Butter and Jelly Fudge will make anyone's taste buds smile! The creamy candy, topped with strawberry preserves, is easy to make — with almost no cooking. To dress up purchased gift bags for Valentine's Day, accent our heart-shaped tags with silk flowers and satin bows.

PEANUT BUTTER AND JELLY FUDGE

4¹/₂ cups sifted confectioners sugar

 2 cups graham cracker crumbs

 1 cup creamy peanut butter

 1 cup butter or margarine, melted

 1 package (10 ounces) peanut butter chips

 ¹/₃ cup strawberry preserves

In a large bowl, combine confectioners sugar, cracker crumbs, peanut butter, and butter; stir until well blended. Line a 9 x 13-inch baking pan with a double layer of aluminum foil, extending foil over ends of pan; grease foil. Press mixture into pan.

For topping, place peanut butter chips in a small microwave-safe bowl. Microwave on high power (100%) 1 minute; stir. Continue to microwave until chips begin to melt, stirring every 15 seconds. Stir until smooth. Spread melted chips over peanut butter mixture. Using edges of foil, immediately lift peanut butter mixture from pan. Spread preserves over melted chips. Cut into 1-inch squares. Store in an airtight container in refrigerator.

Yield: about 8 dozen pieces fudge

For each heart tag, trace large and small heart patterns, page 120, onto tracing paper; cut out. Follow manufacturer's instructions to fuse paper-backed fusible web to wrong side of a 6" square of fabric and a 3" square of cream-colored paper. Fuse fabric to poster board. Use large heart pattern to cut heart from fabric-covered poster board; use small heart pattern to cut heart from cream-colored paper. Fuse small heart to center of large heart. Use a black felt-tip pen with fine point to draw dots and dashes around edge of heart to resemble stitching and to write message on heart. Hot glue silk flowers and a bow tied from 1/8"w satin ribbon to heart. Glue tag to purchased bag.

HUGS AND KISSES COOKIES

*Y*our loved ones will think you're the sweetest person they know when you share these Valentine Cookies. Made from sugar cookie mix, the treats are deliciously easy to create. Simply roll out the dough, cut into heart shapes, bake, and decorate with purchased icing! Pizza take-out boxes covered with wrapping paper and adorned with doilies, paper lace, and satin bows become lovely gift containers for your sentimental surprises.

VALENTINE COOKIES

    1 package (15 ounces) sugar
          cookie mix
    1 egg
       Red decorating icing

Use heart patterns, page 120, and follow Tracing Patterns, page 122. Preheat oven to 375 degrees. In a medium bowl, combine sugar cookie mix and egg; stir until thoroughly moistened. Form dough into a ball. Lightly grease a 14-inch sheet of aluminum foil; place on a damp counter. Use a floured rolling pin to roll out dough to 1/4-inch thickness on foil. Leaving 1 inch between cookies, place patterns on dough and use a sharp knife to cut out hearts. Remove dough scraps. Place foil with cookies on baking sheet. Bake cookies 10 to 12 minutes or until bottoms of cookies are lightly browned. Transfer cookies on foil to wire rack; allow to cool for 2 minutes. Using a large spatula, remove cookies from foil and place on a wire rack to cool completely. Place decorating icing in pastry bag fitted with a small round tip. Pipe desired decorations on cookies.

Yield: four 7 1/2-inch cookies or nine 4 1/2-inch cookies

For each box, follow Gift Box instructions, page 122, to cover box with wrapping paper. We covered pizza take-out boxes and used craft glue to glue paper lace, doilies, and satin bows to the boxes.

TREATS FOR "SOMEBUNNY"

*I*t's easy to delight a special "somebunny" with this Easter treat! First you make the cutout sugar cookies using refrigerated dough; then fill fun-to-use squeeze bottles with pastel icing so your friend can decorate the cookies. For delivery, pack undecorated cookies in our clever Easter Bunny bag and tuck it in a roomy basket along with the bottles of icing.

SPRINGTIME COOKIES

- 1 package (20 ounces) refrigerated sugar cookie dough
- 3 cups sifted confectioners sugar
- 1/3 cup milk
- 1/2 teaspoon almond extract

  Yellow, blue, pink, green, and purple paste food coloring and 6 small-tipped squeeze bottles to decorate

Preheat oven to 350 degrees. Roll out cookie dough according to sugar cookie package directions. Use desired cookie cutters (we used bunny, egg, flower, and baby chick cutters) to cut out cookies. Bake 5 to 7 minutes or until edges are light brown. Transfer to a wire rack to cool.

For icing, combine sugar, milk, and almond extract until smooth. Place 4 tablespoons icing in each of five small bowls and tint with food coloring. Pour each color of icing into a separate squeeze bottle. Pour remaining white icing into remaining bottle. Store cookies in an airtight container.

Yield: about 6 dozen cookies

BUNNY BAG

You will need a 6" x 11" pink paper bag, white poster board, tracing paper, three 8" purple pipe cleaners, 1½" pink pom-pom, two 7/8" dia. wiggle eyes, pink colored pencil, black felt-tip pen with medium point, drawing compass, hot glue gun, and glue sticks.

1. Trace teeth and ear patterns onto tracing paper; cut out. Use patterns to cut teeth and 2 ears from poster board. For cheeks, cut two 2¾" dia. circles from poster board.
2. Use pink pencil to color insides of ears; use pen to outline teeth.
3. For face, overlap cheeks ½" and glue together. Glue teeth to back of cheeks at bottom. Cross centers of pipe cleaners to form whiskers; glue to center of cheeks. Glue pom-pom to center of whiskers for nose. Glue eyes to tops of cheeks.
4. For flap, fold top of bag 3" to front. Glue face to flap. Glue bottom of each ear to back of bag. Fold tip of 1 ear forward.

EAR

TEETH

A LOVING GIFT

*F*or Mother's Day, a jar of our soothing Caribbean Tea Mix conveys a heartfelt message of love. Our sweet jar topper is created by using colored pencils to draw a pretty floral design on a Battenberg lace doily. A soft ribbon holds the doily in place and keeps a spoon handy for stirring. A little cluster of flowers enhances its feminine appeal. Present this thoughtful gift to Mom as a small token of your affection. As she sips the tropical-tasting tea, she'll still feel extra special long after Mother's Day has passed.

CARIBBEAN TEA MIX

2 cups unsweetened powdered instant tea
2 packages (3 ounces each) orange-pineapple-flavored gelatin
1 cup sugar
3/4 teaspoon coconut extract

In a food processor, combine all ingredients. Process until well blended. Store in an airtight container. Give with serving instructions.

Yield: about 3 cups tea mix

To serve: Stir 2 level tablespoons tea mix into 6 ounces hot water.

LACY CANISTER COVER

You will need a 5 1/2"h x 4" dia. glass canister; a 10" dia. doily with Battenberg lace trim; brown ink pen with very fine point; yellow, light pink, dark pink, blue, and green colored pencils; 30" of 1/4"w dark pink satin ribbon; pink plastic spoon; dark pink paint pen; polyester bonded batting; small silk flowers with leaves; hot glue gun; and glue sticks.

1. Center doily right side up over pattern. Use brown pen to trace design onto doily. Use colored pencils to color design.
2. Use top of canister lid as a pattern to cut a circle of batting. Fill canister with tea mix. Place lid on canister. Place batting on lid.
3. Thread ribbon through lace along edge of doily. Place doily on lid of canister over batting and pull ribbon to gather doily around lid. Tie ribbon ends into a bow.
4. Glue flowers and leaves above bow.
5. Use paint pen to write "HAPPY MOTHER'S DAY" on spoon. Allow to dry. Tuck spoon handle behind ribbon.

TEX-MEX PICNIC PLEASER

KETCHUP BAG

For bag to hold a 17-ounce bottle, you will need a 5¹/₂" x 21¹/₂" piece of fabric for bag, thread to match fabric, a 7" square of fabric for stars, two 24" lengths of jute twine, white poster board, tracing paper, paper-backed fusible web, hole punch, craft glue, and a red felt-tip pen with fine point.

1. For bag, follow Steps 2 - 4 of Fabric Bag instructions, page 122.
2. Follow manufacturer's instructions to fuse web to wrong side of star fabric.
3. Trace patterns onto tracing paper; cut out. Use star patterns to cut stars from fabric. Use banner pattern to cut banner from poster board.
4. Fuse small star to front of bag.
5. For tag, fuse large star to poster board; cut out. Glue 1 end of banner to back of large star. Use pen to write "HAPPY MEMORIAL DAY!" on banner. Punch hole at top of star. Tie lengths of twine together around top of bag. Thread tag onto ends of twine. Tie ends into a bow. Knot ends of each streamer.

*M*emorial Day is a nice time to relax with family and friends and enjoy an outdoor picnic. At your next neighborhood cookout, surprise the chef with a bottle of saucy Tex-Mex Ketchup. Made by blending ketchup, salsa, and spices, the quick-and-easy condiment is great with hamburgers, hot dogs, and other picnic fare. Tuck a bottle of the ketchup in your patriotic bag for a real crowd pleaser.

TEX-MEX KETCHUP

1 cup medium-hot thick and
   chunky salsa
1 tablespoon dried cilantro
1 teaspoon ground cumin
1 teaspoon dried minced onion
1 bottle (32 ounces) ketchup

In a medium bowl, combine all ingredients; stir until well blended. Store in an airtight container in refrigerator.
Yield: about 5 cups ketchup

STARS AND STRIPES MUFFINS

Crowned with a fluffy swirl of red, white, and blue icing, Stars and Stripes Muffins have all-American appeal! The sweet treats are especially nice for sharing with schoolchildren on Flag Day or any public-spirited holiday. Easily prepared with blueberry muffin mix, each patriotic pastry hides a cherry surprise inside! For a presentation that displays your love of country, top each muffin with a tiny American flag.

STARS AND STRIPES MUFFINS

MUFFINS
- 1 package (14 ounces) blueberry muffin mix, and ingredients required to prepare muffins
- 1/2 cup cherry preserves

ICING
- 3 cups sifted confectioners sugar
- 1/3 cup vegetable shortening
- 1 1/2 teaspoons clear vanilla extract
- 2 tablespoons milk
  Red and blue paste food coloring
  Small flags to decorate

Preheat oven to 400 degrees. For muffins, mix according to package directions. Place 1 tablespoon batter in foil muffin cups or in each cup of a greased and floured muffin tin. Spoon 1 teaspoon cherry preserves into center of batter. Top with 1 tablespoon muffin batter. Bake 16 to 19 minutes or until tops are light brown. Transfer to a wire rack to cool completely.

For icing, combine first 4 ingredients in large bowl; beat until smooth. Use a small paintbrush to paint a stripe of red and a stripe of blue food coloring inside a pastry bag fitted with a large star tip. Spoon icing into pastry bag. Pipe icing onto muffins. Decorate with flags. Store in an airtight container.

Yield: 12 muffins

SUPER-EASY PIES

*A*s easy as 1-2-3.
hat's what you'll say about
hese creamy Black Bottom
ies! For Father's Day, the kids
an prepare these no-fuss,
o-bake delights with just a
ttle help from Mom. Simply
repare instant chocolate and
anilla puddings, layer them
a store-bought chocolate
rumb pie crusts, and cover
ith whipped topping and
hocolate chips. Presented
long with name tags and
reeting cards made by the
hildren, these tasty gifts are
ure to put big smiles on
ad's and Grandpa's faces!

BLACK BOTTOM PIES

  1 package (3.9 ounces) instant
     chocolate pudding and pie
     filling mix
3½ cups cold milk, divided
  2 9-inch purchased chocolate
     crumb pie crusts
  1 package (3.4 ounces) instant vanilla
     pudding and pie filling mix
  1 container (12 ounces) frozen non-
     dairy whipped topping, thawed
½ cup mini chocolate chips, divided

In a medium bowl, beat chocolate pudding mix and 1¾ cups milk for 1 minute. Pour one-half of chocolate pudding into each crust. Place crusts in refrigerator to chill. In a medium bowl, beat vanilla pudding mix and remaining 1¾ cups milk for 1 minute. Pour vanilla pudding over chilled chocolate pudding. Chill for 10 minutes. Spread whipped topping evenly over pies. Sprinkle ¼ cup chocolate chips over each pie. Cover and store in refrigerator.

Yield: two 9-inch pies

AN ALL-AMERICAN TREAT

*T*his all-American treat makes a great gift for the Fourth of July! Bursting with chocolate chips and chopped nuts, chewy Almond Cookie Bars have a sweet, nutty flavor — and they're quick to make in the microwave. The "explosive" container is made by covering a tin canister with patriotic fabric and adding a sparkly "fuse" made from star-spangled metallic garlands.

ALMOND COOKIE BARS

3/4 cup quick-cooking oats
3/4 cup firmly packed brown sugar, divided
1/2 cup butter or margarine, softened
1/4 cup all-purpose flour
1 egg, beaten
1 tablespoon milk
1/2 teaspoon almond extract
1 package (6 ounces) semisweet chocolate chips
1 cup finely chopped pecans, divided

In a medium bowl, combine oats, 1/2 cup brown sugar, butter, flour, egg, milk, and almond extract; stir in chocolate chips and 1/2 cup pecans. Spread batter evenly in a greased 8-inch square microwave-safe baking dish. For topping, combine remaining 1/4 cup brown sugar and remaining 1/2 cup pecans in a small bowl; sprinkle over batter. Lightly press topping into batter. Microwave on high power (100%) 3 minutes; rotate dish. Cook 3 to 5 minutes longer or until sugar topping is melted. Cool completely. Cut into 1 1/2-inch squares. Store in an airtight container.

Yield: about 2 dozen bars

FIRECRACKER CANISTER

You will need a round tin canister with lid (we used a 4 1/2" dia. x 6 1/4"h canister), fabrics to cover canister and lid, polyester bonded batting, 1/4"w gold trim, satin ribbon same width as side of lid, wired star garland, gold wire garland, fabric marking pencil, hammer, nail, spray adhesive, craft glue, spring-type clothespins, hot glue gun, and glue sticks.

1. To cover canister, leave lid on canister and measure from bottom edge of lid to bottom edge of canister. Measure around side of canister; add 1/2". Cut a piece of fabric the determined measurements. Remove lid from canister.

2. Apply spray adhesive to wrong side of fabric. With 1 long edge of fabric along bottom edge of canister, smooth fabric onto canister, overlapping short edges.

3. (*Note:* For remaining steps, use craft glue unless otherwise indicated.) With ends of trim at seam, glue gold trim along top and bottom edges of fabric on canister.

4. To cover lid, use fabric marking pencil to draw around lid on wrong side of fabric. Cut out fabric 1/2" outside pencil line. Clip edge of fabric at 1/2" intervals to within 1/8" of line. Use top of lid as a pattern and cut 1 circle from batting; glue batting to lid. Center fabric circle right side up on lid. Alternating sides and pulling fabric taut, glue clipped edges of fabric to side of lid; secure with clothespins until glue is dry. If necessary, trim edges of fabric just above bottom edge of lid. Measure around side of lid; add 1/2". Cut ribbon the determined measurement. Glue to side of lid.

5. For fuse, use hammer and nail to punch a hole in center of lid. Cut several lengths of each kind of garland. Twist 1 end of garland lengths together; insert twisted ends through hole in center of lid and bend to one side. Hot glue ends to inside of lid to secure.

6. Separate strands of garland. Wrap ends of several garland lengths around a pencil to curl.

BLUE CHEESE POTATO SALAD

*O*ur tangy *Blue Cheese Potato Salad will make a delightfully different side dish for a Labor Day picnic. It's easy to make — simply toss boiled new potatoes with a creamy sauce that's made with bottled dressing and crumbled blue cheese. To share this gourmet summertime fare, pack the salad in a plastic deli container topped with a hand-drawn label.*

BLUE CHEESE POTATO SALAD

- 3 pounds unpeeled new potatoes, quartered
- 1 bottle (8 ounces) creamy blue cheese dressing
- 3/4 cup (4 ounces) crumbled blue cheese
- 1 jar (2 ounces) real bacon pieces
- 1 tablespoon dried parsley flakes
- 1 tablespoon dried sweet pepper flakes
- 1 teaspoon ground black pepper
- 1 teaspoon dried chopped onion

Place potatoes in a large saucepan and cover with salted water. Bring to a boil and cook until potatoes are tender; drain and rinse with cold water to stop cooking process. In a large bowl, combine remaining ingredients; stir in potatoes. Cover and refrigerate 2 hours to allow flavors to blend. Serve chilled.

Yield: about 9 cups potato salad

For salad container, use lid from a plastic deli container as a pattern to cut a piece from light brown handmade paper (available at art stores); trim paper to fit on top of lid. Use brown felt-tip pen with fine point to draw outlines of potatoes on pape Use blue paint pen to write "BLUE CHEESE POTATO SALAD" on paper; allow to dry. U brown pen to shade letters. Use spray adhesive to glue paper to lid.

HONEY OF A DIP

*I*magine crunchy apples or other fresh fruit served with our creamy Honey-Cinnamon Fruit Dip. What a delightful treat for Labor Day — or any day! The tasty dip whips up in an instant and looks especially appealing when packaged in a jar dressed up with jute and ribbon. For delivery, line a basket with a red checkered cloth and add lots of fresh fruit for snacking.

HONEY-CINNAMON FRUIT DIP

1 package (8 ounces) cream cheese, softened
1 jar (7 ounces) marshmallow creme
1 tablespoon honey
1/4 teaspoon ground cinnamon
   Fresh fruit to serve

In a small bowl, combine all ingredients. Beat on low speed of an electric mixer until smooth. Store in an airtight container in refrigerator. Serve with fresh fruit.

Yield: about 1 1/2 cups dip

FRIGHTFULLY EASY TOFFEE

*T*reat goblins of all
ages to a frightfully special
Halloween surprise with
this scrumptious Microwave
Butter Toffee! Topped with
creamy chocolate and rich
walnuts, the buttery candy
will have every ghoul grinning
with delight. An eye-catching
appliquéd jack-o'-lantern tin
is the perfect container for
your gift.

MICROWAVE BUTTER TOFFEE

1¹/₃ cups sugar
1 cup butter, softened
2 tablespoons water
1 tablespoon dark corn syrup
1 teaspoon vanilla extract
³/₄ cup semisweet chocolate chips
²/₃ cup chopped walnuts

In a large microwave-safe bowl, mix
sugar, butter, water, and corn syrup.
Microwave on high power (100%)
minutes; stir. Stirring every 2 minutes,
microwave 6 to 8 minutes longer or until
mixture thickens and turns golden. Stir in
vanilla. Pour mixture into an ungreased
x 13-inch baking pan. Sprinkle chocolate
chips over hot toffee; spread with a spatula.
Before chocolate hardens, sprinkle with
walnuts. Cool completely. Break into pieces.
Store in an airtight container.

Yield: about 1¹/₄ pounds of candy

JACK-O'-LANTERN TIN

You will need a tin with lid that measures at
least 4¹/₂" x 7"; black spray paint; black
fabric to cover lid; polyester bonded batting;
grosgrain ribbon and metallic trim to cover
side of lid; orange and green lamé fabrics
for appliqué; black glitter, orange, and
green dimensional paints in squeeze bottles;
paper-backed fusible web; satin ribbons;
fabric marking pencil; spring-type
clothespins; craft glue; hot glue gun; and
glue sticks.

1. Spray paint tin and lid black; allow to dry.
2. For fabric to cover lid, use fabric marking
pencil to draw around lid on wrong side of
black fabric. Cut out fabric ¹/₂" outside
pencil line. Clip edges of fabric at ¹/₂"
intervals to within ¹/₈" of line.
3. For appliqué, trace jack-o'-lantern and
stem patterns onto paper side of web;
leaving space around each shape, cut out.
Follow manufacturer's instructions to fuse
web shapes to wrong sides of appliqué
fabrics. Cut out each shape along drawn
lines and remove paper backing. Arrange

jack-o'-lanterns and stems at center on
right side of black fabric; fuse in place.
4. (*Note:* Allow to dry after each paint
color.) Use orange paint to outline and
draw detail lines on jack-o'-lanterns. Use
green paint to outline stems. Use black
glitter paint to paint faces on jack-o'-
lanterns.
5. Use top of lid as a pattern to cut 1 piece
from batting; hot glue batting to top of lid.
Center black fabric right side up on lid over
batting. Pulling fabric taut, use craft glue to
glue edges of fabric to sides of lid; secure
with clothespins until glue is dry. If
necessary, trim edges of fabric just above
bottom of lid.
6. To cover side of lid, measure around
side of lid; add ¹/₂". Cut grosgrain ribbon
and metallic trim the determined
measurement. Hot glue ribbon to side of
lid. Hot glue trim along center of ribbon.
7. Form several satin ribbon lengths into
a double-loop bow; tie another ribbon
length around center to secure. Hot glue
bow to lid.

SPOOKY SWEETS

This sweet, colorful Microwave Orange Candied Corn is so effortless to make — it's almost spooky! The crunchy treat is sure to elicit squeals of delight from little goblins. Presented in our ghostly bag, it's perfect for Halloween party favors.

MICROWAVE ORANGE CANDIED CORN

       Vegetable cooking spray
16   cups popped popcorn
 2   cups sugar
¹/₂ cup light corn syrup
 1   tablespoon orange extract
 1   teaspoon salt
 1   teaspoon baking soda
       Orange paste food coloring

Spray inside of a 14 x 20-inch oven cooking bag with cooking spray. Place popcorn in bag. In a 2-quart microwave-safe bowl, combine sugar and corn syrup. Microwave on high power (100%) 2 minutes or until mixture boils. Stir and microwave 2 minutes longer. Stir in orange extract, salt, and baking soda; tint orange. Pour syrup over popcorn; stir and shake until well coated. Microwave on high power 3 minutes, stirring and shaking after each minute. Spread on aluminum foil sprayed with cooking spray. Cool completely. Store in an airtight container.

Yield: about 18 cups candied corn

GHOST BAG

You will need a 6" x 11" white paper bag, 3" dia. plastic foam ball, white tissue paper, orange curling ribbon, bright green paper for tag, 2 rubber bands, and a black felt-tip pen with fine point.

1. Place candied corn in bag. Wrap a rubber band around bag 2" from top.
2. For ghost, open top of bag above rubber band and place foam ball in top of bag. Center two 20" squares of tissue paper over foam ball. Gather paper below foam ball and secure with remaining rubber band. Tie 2 lengths of ribbon into a bow around neck, covering rubber band. Curl ribbon ends.
3. Use pen to draw eyes on face.
4. Cut tag shape from green paper and use pen to write "BOO!!" on tag. Make a small hole in point of tag and thread tag onto ribbon.

BEWITCHING PUNCH

*Y*ou'll stir up a real
*p*arty sensation when you
*s*urprise a friend with this
*s*irited Witches' Brew.
*S*iked with vodka, the
*f*uity drink will bring out
*t*e Halloween "spirit" in
*e*yone! For a hauntingly
*o*riginal presentation, deliver
*t*e goblin-green punch in a
*c*ear glass jar decorated to
*r*semble a grinning witch.

WITCHES' BREW

2 quarts orange juice

3 cups water

1 can (12 ounces) frozen pineapple
juice concentrate, thawed

1/2 cups vodka

1 cup sugar

1 can (6 ounces) frozen limeade
concentrate, thawed

1 package (0.14 ounces) lemon-
lime-flavored soft drink mix

In a 1-gallon container, combine all
ingredients. Cover and refrigerate until well
chilled. Serve over ice.

Yield: about twenty 6-ounce servings

"BE-WITCH-ING" JAR

You will need a 1-gallon clear glass jar with
straight sides; white, yellow, pink, and black
oil-base paint pens; a 7" dia. paper plate; a
child's cone-shaped party hat; metallic
purple paper twist; 1 yd of 1/16"w black satin
ribbon; hot glue gun; glue sticks; black
spray paint; tracing paper; and removable
tape.

1. For face, trace pattern, page 121, onto
tracing paper. Position pattern inside jar
and tape in place.

2. (*Note:* Allow to dry after each paint
color.) Paint wart on nose pink; pupils of
eyes yellow; and teeth, whites of eyes, and
highlights in eyes white. Paint all lines on
face black. Remove pattern from jar.

3. For hat, cut elastic string from party hat.
Glue bottom edge of party hat to center
bottom of paper plate. Spray paint hat and
plate black. Allow to dry.

4. For hair, cut paper twist into 12" lengths;
untwist lengths. Glue lengths along bottom
edge of hat. Make cuts in lengths from
bottom ends to edge of hat to form strands
of hair. Place hat on jar and trim hair at
front for bangs.

5. Cut ribbon in half. Glue 1 end of each
ribbon length to bottom edge on each side
of hat. Knot remaining ends together.

6. Jar must be gently hand washed.

A GIFT TO RELISH

*Y*our Thanksgiving
hostess will be especially
thankful for this flavorful
offering! Our sweet, fruity
Cran-Raspberry Relish is
easily prepared with canned
and frozen ingredients.
To give your gift a pretty
fall look, tuck a jar of
the relish in a basket lined
with excelsior and trimmed
with silk autumn leaves.
The leaf-shaped tag makes
a nice finishing touch.

CRAN-RASPBERRY RELISH

- 1 can (16 ounces) whole berry
cranberry sauce
- 1 jar (12 ounces) raspberry jelly
- 1 package (12 ounces)
unsweetened frozen
raspberries, thawed
- 1 can (11 ounces) mandarin
oranges, drained
- 1 can (8 ounces) crushed
pineapple, drained
- 1 cup sugar
- 2 tablespoons cornstarch
- 1/2 teaspoon ground cinnamon
- 1/4 teaspoon ground allspice

In a large saucepan, combine all
ingredients. Stirring occasionally, cook over
medium heat until sugar dissolves and
mixture begins to boil. Stirring frequently,
cook 5 minutes or until slightly thickened.
Cool to room temperature. Store in an
airtight container in refrigerator. Serve with
meat, bread, or pound cake.

Yield: about 6 cups relish

THANKSGIVING BASKET

You will need a small basket; wood
excelsior; silk leaves; hot glue gun; glue
sticks; cream-colored paper for tag; black
felt-tip pen with fine point; 20" each of
brown, orange, and rust 1/16"w satin ribbon;
and a hole punch.
For jar lid insert, you will *also* need fabric,
polyester bonded batting, lightweight
cardboard, and craft glue.

1. Hot glue leaves to rim and bottom of
basket. Line basket with excelsior.
2. For tag, draw around a leaf on paper; cut
out leaf 1/8" inside drawn line. Use pen to
write "HAPPY THANKSGIVING" on tag. Place
tag on top of leaf and punch a hole through
both. Thread tag and leaf onto ribbons; tie
ribbons into a bow around basket handle.
3. For jar lid insert, follow Jar Lid Finishing,
page 122.

FRUITFUL HARVEST

*C*elebrate the harvest
season with our fruitful
orange Spice Bread. The
enticing loaves are easily
made from bran muffin mix
flavored with marmalade,
allspice, and raisins. The
recipe yields four gift loaves,
and each can be presented in
our fabric-covered bag
trimmed with ribbon and
dried flowers. These autumn
offerings are sure to reap
plenty of compliments.

ORANGE SPICE BREAD

    2 packages (7 ounces each) bran
          muffin mix
 ¹/₂ cup raisins
    2 eggs
 ¹/₂ cup orange juice concentrate,
          thawed
 ¹/₂ cup orange marmalade, divided
    4 tablespoons vegetable oil
 ¹/₄ cup milk
    2 teaspoons ground allspice

Preheat oven to 400 degrees. In a
medium bowl, combine muffin mix and
raisins. Add eggs, orange juice concentrate,
tablespoons orange marmalade, oil, milk,
and allspice; stir until well-blended. Pour
into 4 greased and floured 3¹/₄ x 5³/₄-inch
loaf pans. Bake 20 to 25 minutes or until a
toothpick inserted in center comes out
clean. Remove loaves from pans and place
on wire rack. Spread remaining orange
marmalade evenly over tops of hot loaves.
Cool completely. Store in an airtight
container.

Yield: 4 mini loaves bread

FABRIC-COVERED BAG

You will need a paper bag, fabric, paper-
backed fusible web, 13" of 1³/₈"w wired
ribbon, dried flowers, hole punch, craft
glue, hot glue gun, and glue sticks.

1. Carefully pull bag apart at seams and
spread flat. Cut a piece of fabric slightly
larger on all sides than unfolded bag.
2. Following manufacturer's instructions,
fuse web to wrong side of fabric; fuse fabric
to right side of unfolded bag. Trim fabric
even with edges of bag.

3. Refold bag along previously folded lines.
Use craft glue to glue bag back together.
Allow to dry.
4. Place loaf of bread wrapped in plastic
wrap in bag. Fold top of bag 2" to back.
5. For bow, punch 2 holes 1" apart near top
fold of bag; thread ribbon ends through
holes and tie into a bow. Hot glue flowers to
center of bow.

HOLIDAY BREAKFAST ROLLS

*H*ere's a gift that's perfect for Christmas morning when there's no time to cook a big breakfast! Quickie Cinnamon Rolls, made with canned biscuits and a buttery brown sugar topping, are simple to prepare and deliver a day or two ahead, ready to bake in an aluminum cake pan. Stocking-shaped ornaments trimmed with personalized cuffs and jingle bells make great gift tags and can be used as cheery tree-trimmers for years to come.

QUICKIE CINNAMON ROLLS

- 3/4 cup firmly packed brown sugar
- 1/4 cup butter or margarine
- 1 teaspoon ground cinnamon
- 1/4 cup chopped pecans
- 1 can (10 biscuits) refrigerated Texas-style biscuits

In a small saucepan over medium heat, stir brown sugar, butter, and cinnamon until butter melts. Pour butter mixture into a 9-inch round cake pan. Sprinkle pecans over butter mixture. Dip one side of each biscuit in mixture; place coated side up in pan. Cover and refrigerate (best if baked and eaten within 1 to 2 days). Give with serving instructions.

Yield: 10 cinnamon rolls

To serve: Bake uncovered in a preheated 400-degree oven 12 to 18 minutes or until bread is light brown. Serve immediately.

STOCKING ORNAMENTS

For each ornament, you will need a 4" x 6" print fabric piece for stocking, a 2" x 3½" solid fabric piece for cuff, paper-backed fusible web, heavy paper, a 14" strand of raffia, ½" jingle bell, brown permanent felt-tip pen with fine point, tracing paper, hot glue gun, and glue sticks.

1. Follow manufacturer's instructions to fuse web to wrong sides of fabric pieces. Fuse each fabric piece to a piece of heavy paper.
2. Trace stocking and cuff patterns, page 121, onto tracing paper; cut out. Use patterns to cut stocking and cuff from fabric-covered paper.
3. Glue cuff to top of stocking.
4. Cut raffia strand in half. Thread bell onto 1 length of raffia and tie into a bow; glue to front of stocking.
5. For hanger, knot ends of remaining raffia length together; glue knot to back of stocking.
6. Use pen to write name on cuff.

"CRISP-MAS" CRUNCH BARS

*S*end wishes for a Merry "Crisp-mas" with these delicious Cinnamon Crunch Bars! They're amazingly easy to make by pouring a praline mixture over cinnamon graham crackers topped with chopped walnuts. You'll want to bake several batches to share with friends — and your own family, too! For delivery, pack the treats in a purchased papier mâché bag trimmed with festive greenery, cinnamon sticks, and a fabric bow.

CINNAMON CRUNCH BARS

12 cinnamon graham crackers
      (2¹/₂ x 4³/₄ inches each)
2 cups finely chopped walnuts
1 cup butter
1 cup firmly packed brown sugar
¹/₂ teaspoon ground cinnamon

Preheat oven to 400 degrees. Arrange cinnamon graham crackers in a single layer with sides touching in bottom of a greased 10 x 15-inch jellyroll pan. Sprinkle walnuts evenly over crackers.

In a heavy small saucepan, combine butter, brown sugar, and cinnamon. Stirring constantly, cook over medium heat until sugar dissolves and mixture begins to boil. Continue to boil syrup 3 minutes longer without stirring; pour over crackers. Bake 8 to 10 minutes or until bubbly and slightly darker around the edges. Cool completely in pan. Break into pieces. Store in an airtight container.

Yield: about 1¹/₂ pounds candy

FESTIVE FRUITCAKE

*F*ruitcake has never tasted so good — or been prepared so easily! Start with a box of white cake mix and stir in a few goodies such as candied fruit and chopped pecans. In no time you'll have two loaves of moist, rich, and chewy White Fruitcake! We've wrapped each one in clear cellophane embellished with bendable ribbon and decorative fruit — the perfect gift to herald the holiday season.

WHITE FRUITCAKE

  1 package (18.25 ounces) white
      cake mix
$^2/_3$ cup vegetable oil
$^1/_2$ cup sweetened condensed milk
  2 egg whites
$1^1/_2$ cups chopped candied fruit
$1^1/_2$ cups chopped pecans

Preheat oven to 350 degrees. In a large bowl, beat cake mix, oil, condensed milk, and egg whites on low speed of an electric mixer until moistened; increase to high speed for 2 minutes. Stir in fruit and pecans. Spoon batter into 2 greased and floured 5 x 9-inch baking pans. Bake 40 to 45 minutes or until a toothpick inserted in center of cake comes out clean. Cool in pans 10 minutes. Remove from pans and cool completely on a wire rack. Store in an airtight container.

Yield: 2 loaves fruitcake

BRANDIED CHRISTMAS CHERRIES

BRANDIED CHRISTMAS CHERRIES

1 pound candied whole green
   and red cherries
¹⁄₄ cup diced crystallized ginger
1 cinnamon stick
¹⁄₂ teaspoon whole cloves
¹⁄₂ teaspoon whole allspice
³⁄₄ cup cherry brandy
³⁄₄ cup light corn syrup

Combine cherries and ginger in a
1-quart jar with lid. Place cinnamon stick in
cherry mixture. Place cloves and allspice in
a small piece of cheesecloth or coffee filter;
tie with a string. Place in jar. In a small
bowl, combine brandy and corn syrup; pour
over cherry mixture. Allow to sit at room
temperature for 3 weeks; discard spices.
Store in an airtight container at room
temperature. Serve with cake, ice cream, or
meat dishes.

Yield: about 3 cups fruit

Note: If making jar lid insert, store fruit in
wide-mouth canning jar.

*I*f the holiday rush has a
friend feeling down, why not
remedy the situation with a
jar of our Brandied Christmas
Cherries! Simply combine red
and green candied cherries
with brandy and spices, and
soon you'll have a spirited
sauce that's sure to recapture
that festive mood! It's great
with cake, ice cream, and
even meat dishes. To deliver
your gift basket, put the fruit
mixture in a jar topped with a
cross-stitched lid and include
a bakeshop pound cake.
Matching gift tags are a nice
way to dress up your surprise.

Leaving 1" around design on all sides,
work desired design on Natural
perforated paper (14 ct) using 2
strands of floss for Cross Stitch, 2 for
Backstitch lettering, and 1 for all other
Backstitch. For jar lid insert, center ring
of lid over stitched piece. Use a pencil to
lightly draw around ring. Cut perforated
paper just inside drawn line. Cut a piece
of cream-colored paper same size as
stitched piece. Place stitched piece, then
paper circle, inside jar lid. For each gift
tag, follow grey cutting lines on chart to
cut out stitched piece. Glue tag to a
piece of cream-colored paper. Trim
paper to ¹⁄₈" from edge of stitched
piece.

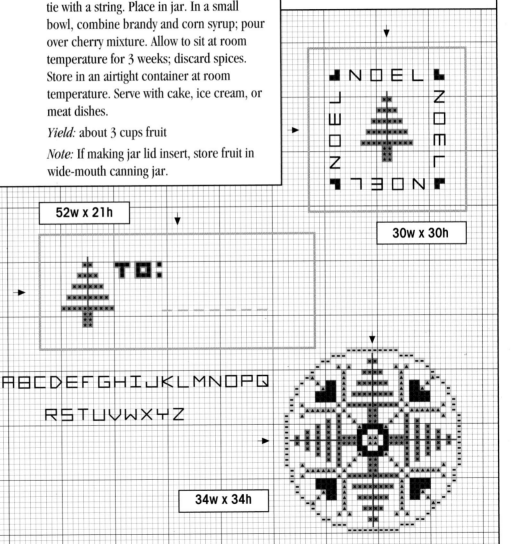

52w x 21h

30w x 30h

34w x 34h

**JAR LID INSERT AND
GIFT TAGS**

X	DMC	B'ST
	310	✎
★	435	
■	498	✎
	500	✎
✖	502	
▬	725	
▲	3755	
✎	cutting line	

CHRISTMAS "CANDY" CHEESECAKE

*O*ur Chocolate-Mint Cheesecake makes a divine holiday gift! The easy recipe makes two, so you can share with a friend and still have one on hand for unexpected company. For a clever presentation, a circle of poster board is decorated to resemble a peppermint candy and placed in the clear lid of a disposable pie carrier. A wrapping of cellophane and ribbons completes the look of a giant Christmas candy.

CHOCOLATE-MINT CHEESECAKES

CRUST

   2 cups chocolate sandwich cookie crumbs (about 22 cookies)
  1/2 cup butter or margarine, melted
   6 tablespoons sugar

FILLING

   3 packages (8 ounces each) cream cheese, softened
   1 can (14 ounces) sweetened condensed milk
   3 eggs
   1 tablespoon vanilla extract
  1/2 cup crushed peppermint candies (about 20 round candies)

Preheat oven to 375 degrees. For crust, combine crumbs, butter, and sugar in a medium bowl. Press mixture into bottom and up sides of 2 greased 9-inch aluminum foil pie pans. Bake 6 to 8 minutes. Remove from oven. Reduce heat to 300 degrees. In a large bowl, beat cream cheese, condensed milk, eggs, and vanilla until well blended. Stir in candies. Pour mixture into crusts. Bake 25 to 30 minutes or until set in center. Cool completely. Store in an airtight container in refrigerator.

Yield: two 9-inch cheesecakes

"PEPPERMINT" CHEESECAKE CARRIER

For each carrier, you will need a clear plastic lid to fit a 9" dia. aluminum foil pie pan (we purchased our pan and lid from a grocery store bakery), poster board, red paper, tracing paper, clear cellophane, red and white curling ribbon, drawing compass, craft glue, and transparent tape.

1. For peppermint shape, cut a 7 1/2" dia. circle from poster board. For stripes, trace stripe pattern onto tracing paper; cut out. Use pattern to cut 5 stripes from red paper. Glue stripes to poster board circle.
2. If necessary, trim peppermint shape to fit inside top of lid. Tape peppermint shape inside top of lid. Place lid on pie pan.
3. Wrap pie pan in cellophane to resemble a peppermint candy; tie lengths of ribbon into bows around ends of cellophane. Curl ribbon ends.

PATTERNS

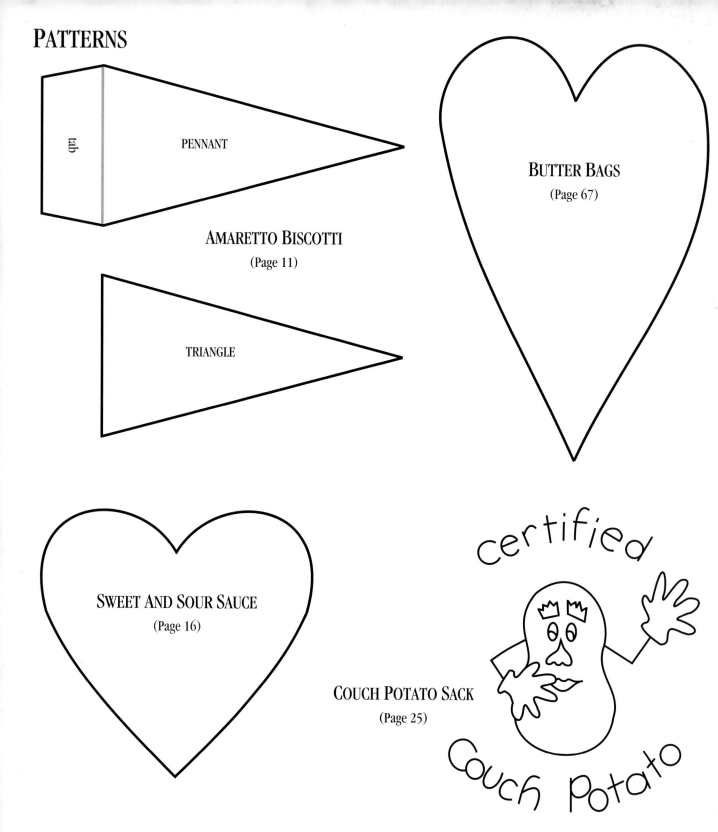

tab

PENNANT

AMARETTO BISCOTTI

(Page 11)

TRIANGLE

BUTTER BAGS

(Page 67)

SWEET AND SOUR SAUCE

(Page 16)

COUCH POTATO SACK

(Page 25)

certified

Couch Potato

CHOCOLATE LOVER'S CAP
(Page 10)

TOASTY BASKET

(Page 79)

PEOPLE CHOW

(Page 80)

119

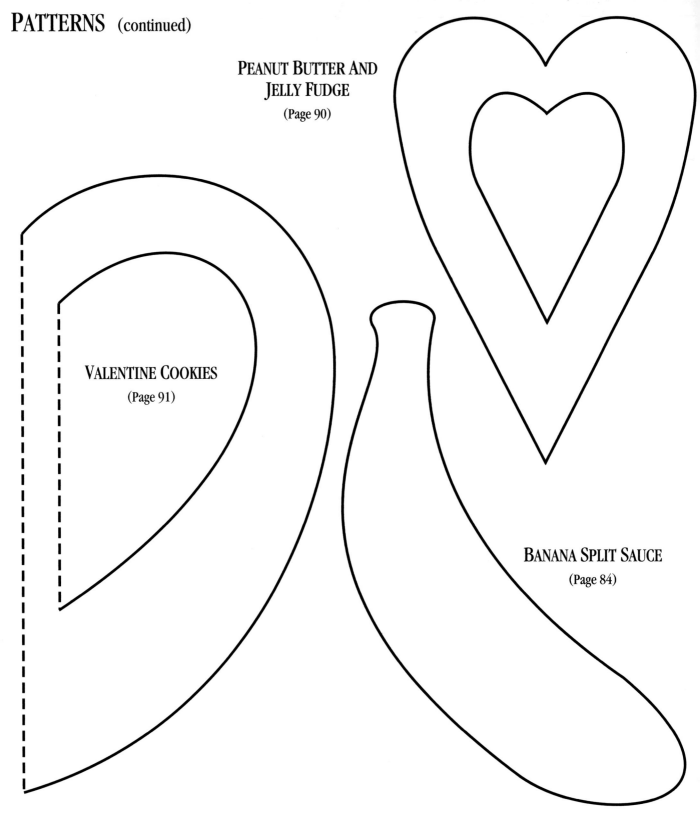

PEANUT BUTTER AND
JELLY FUDGE
(Page 90)

VALENTINE COOKIES
(Page 91)

BANANA SPLIT SAUCE
(Page 84)

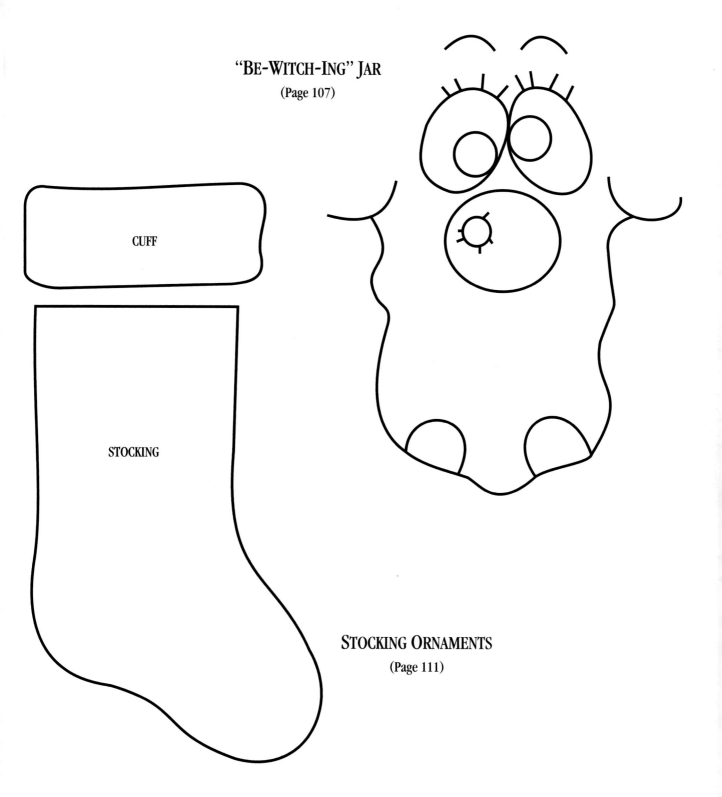

"Be-Witch-Ing" Jar
(Page 107)

CUFF

STOCKING

Stocking Ornaments
(Page 111)

GENERAL INSTRUCTIONS

TRACING PATTERNS

When one-half of pattern (indicated by dashed line on pattern) is shown, fold tracing paper in half and place fold along dashed line of pattern. Trace pattern half, including all placement symbols and markings; turn folded paper over and draw over all markings. Unfold pattern and lay flat. Cut out pattern.

When entire pattern is shown, place tracing paper over pattern and trace pattern, including all placement symbols and markings. Cut out pattern.

LAYERED TAG

Glue a 5" square of fabric or wrapping paper to a 5" square of heavy paper. For tag center, cut paper desired size. Glue tag center to center of covered paper. Trim covered paper 1/8" to 1/2" from tag center.

EASY BASKET LINER

Cut fabric square 1/2" larger on all sides than desired finished size of liner. Follow manufacturer's instructions to fuse 1/2"w paper-backed fusible web tape along 1 edge on wrong side of fabric square. Do not remove paper backing. Press edge to wrong side along inner edge of tape. Unfold edge and remove paper backing. Refold edge and fuse in place. Repeat for remaining edges.

FABRIC BAG

1. To determine width of fabric needed, add 1/2" to finished width of bag. To determine length of fabric needed, double finished height of bag and add 1 1/2". Cut fabric the determined measurements.
2. With right sides together and matching short edges, fold fabric in half; finger press folded edge (bottom of bag). Using a 1/4" seam allowance and thread to match fabric, sew sides of bag together.

3. Press top edge of bag 1/4" to wrong side; press 1/2" to wrong side again and stitch in place.
4. For bag with flat bottom, match each side seam to fold line at bottom of bag; sew across each corner 1" from point (Fig. 1). Turn bag right side out.

Fig. 1

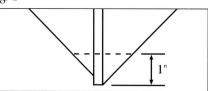

STENCILING

1. For first stencil, cut a piece of acetate 1" larger on all sides than entire pattern. Center acetate over pattern and use permanent felt-tip pen with fine point to trace outlines of all areas of first color in stencil cutting key. For placement guidelines, use dashed lines to outline remaining colored areas. Using a new piece of acetate for each color in stencil cutting key, repeat for remaining stencils.
2. Place each acetate piece on cutting mat and use craft knife to cut out stencil along solid lines, making sure edges are smooth.
3. (*Note:* If desired, use removable tape to mask any cutout areas on stencil next to area being painted.) Hold or tape first stencil in place. Use a clean dry stencil brush for each color of paint. Referring to color key, dip brush in paint and remove excess on paper towel. Brush should be almost dry to produce good results. Beginning at edge of cutout area, apply paint in a stamping motion to designated areas of design. If indicated in key, shade design by stamping a darker shade of paint in cutout area. Repeat until all areas of first stencil have been painted. Carefully remove stencil; allow paint to dry.

4. Using stencils in order indicated in stencil cutting key and matching guidelines on stencils to previously stenciled areas, repeat Step 3 for remaining stencils.

JAR LID FINISHING

1. For jar lid insert, use flat part of a jar lid (same size as jar lid used in storing food) as a pattern and cut 1 circle each from cardboard, batting, and fabric. Matching edges, use craft glue to glue batting to cardboard. Center fabric circle right side up on batting; glue edge of fabric to batting.
2. Just before presenting gift, remove screw ring from filled jar; place jar lid insert in screw ring and screw in place over lid. If jar has been sealed in canning, be careful not to break seal of lid. If seal of lid is broken, jar must be refrigerated.

GIFT BOX

Note: Use this technique to cover cardboard boxes that are unassembled or are easily unfolded, such as pie boxes.

1. Unfold box to be covered. Cut a piece of wrapping paper 1" larger on all sides than unfolded box. Place wrapping paper right side down on a flat surface.
2. For a small box, apply spray adhesive to outside of entire box. Center unfolded box, adhesive side down, on paper; press firmly to secure.
3. For a large box, apply spray adhesive to bottom of box. Center unfolded box, adhesive side down, on paper; press firmly to secure. Applying spray adhesive to 1 section at a time, repeat to secure remaining sections of box to paper.
4. Use a craft knife to cut paper even with edges of box. If box has slits, use craft knife to cut through slits from inside of box.
5. Reassemble box.

CROSS STITCH

COUNTED CROSS STITCH (X)

Work 1 Cross Stitch to correspond to each colored square on the chart. For horizontal rows, work stitches in 2 journeys (Fig. 1). For vertical rows, complete each stitch as shown in Fig. 2. When the chart shows a Backstitch crossing a colored square (Fig. 3), a Cross Stitch (Fig. 1 or 2) should be worked first; then the Backstitch (Fig. 5) should be worked on top of the Cross Stitch.

Fig. 1

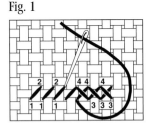

Fig. 2

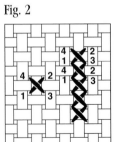

Fig. 3

QUARTER STITCH (¼X)

Quarter Stitches are denoted by triangular shapes of color in chart and color key. Come up at 1 (Fig. 4); then split fabric thread to go down at 2.

Fig. 4

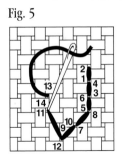

BACKSTITCH (B'ST)

For outline detail, Backstitch (shown in chart and color key by black or colored straight lines) should be worked after the design has been completed (Fig. 5).

Fig. 5

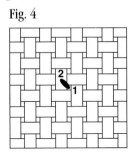

FRENCH KNOT

Bring needle up at 1. Wrap floss once around needle and insert needle at 2, holding end of floss with non-stitching fingers (Fig. 6). Tighten knot; then pull needle through fabric, holding floss until it must be released. For a larger knot, use more strands; wrap only once.

Fig. 6

PLASTIC CANVAS

TENT STITCH

This stitch is worked over 1 intersection as shown in Fig. 1.

Fig. 1

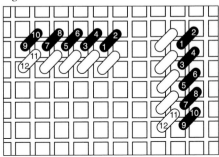

OVERCAST STITCH

This stitch covers the edge of the canvas (Fig. 2). It may be necessary to go through the same hole more than once to get an even coverage on the edge, especially at the corners.

Fig. 2

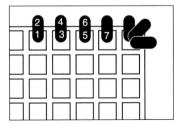

KITCHEN TIPS

MEASURING INGREDIENTS

Liquid measuring cups have a rim above the measuring line to keep liquid ingredients from spilling. Nested measuring cups are used to measure dry ingredients, butter, shortening, and peanut butter. Measuring spoons are used for measuring both dry and liquid ingredients.

To measure flour or granulated sugar: Spoon ingredient into nested measuring cup and level off with a knife. Do not pack down with spoon.

To measure confectioners sugar: Sift sugar, spoon lightly into nested measuring cup, and level off with a knife.

To measure brown sugar: Pack sugar into nested measuring cup and level off with a knife. Sugar should hold its shape when removed from cup.

To measure dry ingredients equaling less than 1/4 cup: Dip measuring spoon into ingredient and level off with a knife.

To measure butter, shortening, or peanut butter: Pack ingredient firmly into nested measuring cup and level off with a knife.

To measure liquids: Use a liquid measuring cup placed on a flat surface. Pour ingredient into cup and check measuring line at eye level.

To measure honey or syrup: For a more accurate measurement, lightly spray measuring cup or spoon with cooking spray before measuring so the liquid will release easily from cup or spoon.

SOFTENING BUTTER OR MARGARINE

To soften butter, remove wrapper from butter and place on a microwave-safe plate. Microwave 1 stick 20 to 30 seconds at medium-low power (30%).

SOFTENING CREAM CHEESE

To soften cream cheese, remove wrapper from cream cheese and place on a microwave-safe plate. Microwave 1 to 1 1/2 minutes at medium power (50%) for one 8-ounce package or 30 to 45 seconds for one 3-ounce package.

SUBSTITUTING HERBS

To substitute fresh herbs for dried, use 1 tablespoon fresh chopped herbs for 1/2 teaspoon dried herbs.

WHIPPING CREAM

For greatest volume, chill a glass bowl, beaters, and cream until well chilled before whipping. In warm weather, place chilled bowl over ice while whipping cream.

CUTTING COOKIE SHAPES

To cut out cookie shapes, dip cookie cutter in flour to keep dough from sticking to cutter.

ROLLING OUT PIE DOUGH

Tear off four 24-inch-long pieces of plastic wrap. Overlapping long edges, place two pieces of wrap on a slightly damp, flat surface; smooth out wrinkles. Place dough in center of wrap. Overlapping long edges, use remaining pieces of wrap to cover dough. Use rolling pin to roll out dough 2 inches larger than diameter of pie plate. Remove top pieces of wrap. Invert dough into pie plate. Remove remaining pieces of wrap.

SHREDDING CHEESE

To shred cheese easily, place wrapped cheese in freezer for 10 to 20 minutes before shredding.

TOASTING NUTS

To toast nuts, spread nuts on an ungreased baking sheet. Stirring occasionally, bake 8 to 10 minutes in a preheated 350-degree oven until nuts are slightly darker in color.

TO DISSOLVE DRY YEAST

Use warm water (105 to 115 degrees) when dissolving yeast. Higher temperatures kill yeast and prevent breads from rising properly.

PREPARING CITRUS FRUIT ZEST

To remove outer portion of peel (colored part) from citrus fruits, use a fine grater or fruit zester, being careful not to get white portion which is bitter. Zest is also referred to as grated peel in recipes.

EQUIVALENT MEASUREMENTS

1 tablespoon	=	3 teaspoons
1/8 cup (1 fluid ounce)	=	2 tablespoons
1/4 cup (2 fluid ounces)	=	4 tablespoons
1/3 cup	=	5 1/3 tablespoons
1/2 cup (4 fluid ounces)	=	8 tablespoons
3/4 cup (6 fluid ounces)	=	12 tablespoons
1 cup (8 fluid ounces)	=	16 tablespoons or 1/2 pint
2 cups (16 fluid ounces)	=	1 pint
1 quart (32 fluid ounces)	=	2 pints
1/2 gallon (64 fluid ounces)	=	2 quarts
1 gallon (128 fluid ounces)	=	4 quarts

HELPFUL FOOD EQUIVALENTS

1/2 cup butter	=	1 stick butter
1 square baking chocolate	=	1 ounce chocolate
1 cup chocolate chips	=	6 ounces chocolate chips
2 1/4 cups packed brown sugar	=	1 pound brown sugar
3 1/2 cups unsifted confectioners sugar	=	1 pound confectioners sugar
2 cups granulated sugar	=	1 pound granulated sugar
4 cups all-purpose flour	=	1 pound all-purpose flour
1 cup shredded cheese	=	4 ounces cheese
3 cups sliced carrots	=	1 pound carrots
1/2 cup chopped celery	=	1 rib celery
1/2 cup chopped onion	=	1 medium onion
1 cup chopped green pepper	=	1 large green pepper

RECIPE INDEX

CREDITS

To Magna IV Color Imaging of Little Rock, Arkansas, we say thank you for the superb color reproduction and excellent pre-press preparation.

We want to especially thank photographers Mark Mathews and Ken West of Peerless Photography, Little Rock, Arkansas, and Jerry R. Davis of Jerry Davis Photography, Little Rock, Arkansas, for their time, patience, and excellent work.

To the talented people who helped in the creation of the following recipes and projects in this book, we extend a special word of thanks:

- *Poppy Seed Chicken,* page 23: Allison Holland
- *Lemon Bites,* page 29: Nora Faye Spencer Clift
- *Summertime Coasters,* page 13: Mary Scott
- *"Beary" Jar Lids,* page 19: Jane Chandler
- *Floral Bread Cloth,* page 59: Jorja Hernandez of Kooler Design Studio
- *Cross-Stitched Mug,* page 71: Diane Brakefield
- *Jar Lid Insert and Gift Tags,* page 115: Jane Chandler

A very special word of thanks goes to Vivien Haupt, age 5, for creating the Father's Day drawing shown on page 99.

We extend a sincere thank you to the people who assisted in making and testing the projects in this book: Janet Akins, Marsha Besancon, Kathy Jones, Karen Tyler, Jackie Wright, and Janie Marie Wright.